The Walk

William Blake, *The Traveller hasteth in the Evening,* from *The Gates of Paradise.* Courtesy of the Lessing J. Rosenwald Collection, Library of Congress, Washington, D.C.

THE WALK

Notes on a Romantic Image

By Jeffrey C. Robinson

University of Oklahoma Press
Norman and London

By Jeffrey C. Robinson

Keats: The Myth of the Hero, by Dorothy Van Ghent (ed.) (Princeton, 1983)
Radical Literary Education: A Classroom Experiment with Wordsworth's "Ode" (Madison, 1987)
The Walk: Notes on a Romantic Image (Norman, 1989)

Library of Congress Cataloging-in-Publication Data

Robinson, Jeffrey Cane, 1943–
    The walk : notes on a romantic image.

    Bibliography: p.
    1. English literature—History and criticism.
2. Walking in literature.   3. Romanticism.   4. Walking.
5. American literature—History and criticism.   I. Title.
PR408.W35R64   1989   820'.9'355   88–37876
ISBN 0–8061–2181–5 (alk. paper)

The paper in this book meets the guidelines for permanence and durability of the Committee on Production Guidelines for Book Longevity of the Council on Library Resources, Inc.

To My Children
Samuel Cane Robinson
and
Miriam Kate Robinson

New myths are formed beneath each of our steps.

—Louis Aragon, *Le Paysans de Paris*

Contents

Illustrations

Acknowledgments

I wish to thank the University of Colorado Council on Research and Creative Work for awarding me a Faculty Fellowship in 1986, allowing me time to complete a late stage of this book.

I would also like to thank the Committee on University Scholarly Publications and the Department of English at the University of Colorado for their financial assistance with illustration fees for this book.

Thanks to Robin Martin and Kay Cook for helping to prepare the manuscript for publication. Thanks also to Marje Urban for typing several drafts on short notice.

With my friend Tom Wolf, I have gone "sounding all the way," walking in Denver for hours or hiking in the Rockies for days.

J.C.R.

Denver, Colorado
October, 1988

The Walk

1.

Introduction

I have just returned from a midday walk. It is early October in Denver's Washington Park. The warm air is steeped in sunshine, the sky bright blue without clouds, the leaves on the trees turning to their own autumnal brightness. Looking west from time to time between the trees, I catch the thin gloom of smog dirtying and blurring the view of the Rocky Mountains and reminding me that—on this Tuesday of business—not all is well and not even a walk can make it so.

This park, familiar to me, exists as a set of assumptions in my life on the walk: the nearly naked joggers and the football and volleyball players, lunchers, old fishermen reclining by one of the lakes with their rods resting near them on wooden sticks, the walkers like myself. Sprinkler showers arc across the expansive lawns, elaborate flower beds settle into their end-of-summer dullness, radios send messages and songs out of open car doors. But the sky is new today, the early autumn light, and the oranging and yellowing of trees. These keep me alert to the world through which I pass. Circling through the park, I move on and off an avenue of innocence.

Besides nature and the lives of persons, another trajectory has intervened in my passage: literature, or, more precisely, the need to set in motion—with an introduction—this book you are about to read. So my walk has not been very spontaneous, or "natural," as people say. Or, rather, there was spontaneity, but it rested in the broad bed of commonality between the actual walk, the pleasures of reading, and the subsequent urges toward writing.

Let me add (to support my point about spontaneity) that when I set myself to write this introduction, I first reread Roland Barthes' brief essay "On Reading" (in *The Rustle of Language*). Then I thought of my opening line, "I have just returned from a walk" ("midday" came later), then I took the walk described, and here I am writing. Barthes quotes the writer Roger Laporte: "Reading Proust, Blanchot, Kafka, Artaud gave me no desire to write *on* these authors (not even, I may add, *like* them), but to *write*."[†] This desire is a familiar one; walking literature releases it in me. Barthes goes on to envision this desire as extravagant. "In this perspective, reading is a veritable production: no longer of interior images, of projections, of hallucinations, but literally of *work*: the (consumed) product is reversed into production, into promise, into desire for production, and the chain of desires begins to unroll, each reading being worth the writing it engenders, to infinity."[†] What is this phenomenon, the walk that urges me to write? How have people in the past two hundred years written about it?

The walk is an occasion of limited vulnerability. I offer myself to unpredictable occurrences and impingements. The world flows past my body, which may block, pleasurably or uncomfortably, some sudden cometary intrusion and create a *situation*. But mostly I can modulate the immediacy of random intrusions for the sake of encouraging, unimpeded, the "inner life." Raising the stakes, the walk implies a mixture or an alternation of committed responses and disinterested reflection, or the world on a walk engenders the mental polarity of critical thinking all the way to wonderment. The walker observes things from a distance, and if the power of the object is in some way too compelling, he by definition detaches himself from it by walking on. Yet the walker is in experience, feels and thinks in his movement through time and space, and is reaching out (or can) to the world in time. To deny either side of the walk is to deny half of experience. Living in the Romantic tradition, we tend to deny the historical, time-rich half. Or if we accept it, it is only to deny the other, seductive half. We accept the experience of beauty or of thought but rarely of both together. This is the real subjective complexity in our receptivity to life and art as we observe and experience them. The walker, often encountering everything fresh, is an innocent. But the walker at the same time comes to experience not innocently but full of knowledge and opinions, as a maker of judgments. Interested and disinterested, I, walking, think in the face of what attracts and what repels me. Furthermore, my thoughts and immediate pleasures belong to me in my solitude but also to me as part of an historical community.

When I walk, my mind does not flow like a stream. More literary than that, it works in mixed genres: at times autobiography, polemic, natural description, dialogue, essay, even treatise, story. Sometimes it seems a genre that keeps resisting genre. Sometimes internal pressures or laxities break the integrity of genre. Other times the break comes from the squirrel that will not get off the path, the sprinkler's spray that I must circle around, the old man trudging past in a heavy great coat on this warm day, the vague green lines of algae on lake water.

This vulnerability of the walker might transform into the vulnerability of the writer to the mixing of genres.

Just as the walk is a quintessentially Romantic image, so the mixing of genres produces a quintessentially Romantic metagenre, what Friedrich Schlegel called *Mischgedicht*. The "mixed poem" follows the lead of desire, through which it states the case for freedom in writing. I have written in the following pages commentaries on walking and on the literary history of walking: phenomenological inquiry, autobiographical or genetic touchstones for my relationship to the subject, analyses of literary and visual objects, surveys of types of walkers or particular historical or national literatures of walking, my own writing of a walk.

Though I range through the truly vast and ever-expanding literature of walking, I have eschewed as a goal the frightening lure of comprehensiveness. No one has ever engaged me on the subject of walking literature who has not offered an instance that "simply can't be left out." Instead, let me offer you the occasion to start producing your own instances and memories and perhaps even the writing desire.

This book moves back and forth between an event in walking literature and the history of an image, a "Romantic image." As a history it gains much of its impetus from that half century in European culture usually named the Romantic period, beginning with the American and

French revolutions, a period when writers (e.g., Rousseau, Wordsworth, Hazlitt) often took to the image of walking, either as a subject or as setting. The image of the walk may be said to code the dialectics of wonderment or consolation and critical thought, or of spiritual transcendence or realization and social-historical encounter, or of aesthetic disinterestedness and sensuous engagement. These are dialectics central to Romantic literature and the subsequent cultural debates they have fostered. We live with them today, and modern writers, painters, sculptors, even city planners are influenced by them. My meditation, it follows, does not respect the borders of the historical period but treads into recent times and various genres and media and at one point ambulates outside of the Western tradition altogether (Basho).

Why is the walk quintessentially a Romantic image? It is, I believe, fundamentally spiritual and fundamentally about the acquisition of happiness. The spiritual dimension to the walk surely appears before Romanticism in, for example, Bunyan's *Pilgrim's Progress* and Milton's *Paradise Lost* in the expulsion of Adam and Eve out of Eden, walking into history, and eventually into salvation through the renewed Eden at the end of Christian time. Capitalism, which, of course, predates Romanticism, is concerned with the acquisition of happiness, not by means of religious or philosophical and ascetic discipline but through commerce. In this sense happiness is theoretically available to all, in fact available to those with money. The history of the walk, in literature and painting, tells of the struggle in the modern world to relocate the possibility for individual happiness irrespective of class, race, or gender, to relocate it in the will of the walker. The walk follows the pressure in eighteenth- and nineteenth-century literature toward the democratization of society.

Romanticism from Rousseau on, fundamentally sensitive to the encroachments of an insensitive industrial society upon the lives of individuals, posits an ahistorical self, a life (buried or at least masked by social rituals) that needs to be recovered. For some the walk occasions this recovery of an essential innocence. Wounded or diseased by modern social life, we can walk our way into health: walking is a form of therapy—more extravagantly, of self-realization. At times we experience on the walk a shock of encounter in the world (either blissful and transcendent, in Wordsworth and Baudelaire, or noxious, in Rousseau and Freud). Walking highlights the drama of confrontation between an inner world and an outer world, worlds that exist in relation to each other in varying degrees of compatibility. In the Romanticism of Rousseau, Wordsworth, and Thoreau the inner world at best conforms to the idyll: rural, benignly patriarchal, expansive, comic. Those writers more sympathetic to the diversities of class and change in urban life see the inner world full of strife and competition and fantasy and find these things not an intrusion but an opportunity for observation, judgment, and participation in changing social realities. The dialectic of "the country and the city," to quote the title of Raymond Williams' classic of British cultural and literary criticism, emerges in the literature of walking.

Fundamentally, I believe, the walker is against dualism and divisions. Discrete steps exist on the walk. Beckett's Watt cannot take more than one step without changing direction. The walker always senses the boundary between mental "space for one's wandering" and the impinging and independent world just beyond the edges of the body. Yet the walk is also continuous motion. The pleasure of walking emerges when all the dialectics appear as play. Writing walking, or writing about the walk, turns play into the problem of the history of play, but one (inspired by the walk) can go a step further and extend the problem once again into play. I would like to think of this not as a solipsism but as a meditation with a democratizing, communalizing intention, rather like Keats, linking the walk to the beauty of the spider's web:

> Now it appears to me that almost any Man may like the Spider spin from his own inwards his own airy Citadel—the points of leaves and twigs on which the Spider begins her work are few and she fills the Air with a beautiful circuiting: man should be content with as few points to tip with the fine Webb of his Soul and weave a tapestry empyrean—full of Symbols for his spiritual eye, of softness for his spiritual touch, of space for his wandering of distinctness for his Luxury—But the Minds of Mortals are so different and bent on such diverse Journeys that it may at first appear impossible for any common taste and fellowship to exist between two or three under these suppositions—It is however quite the contrary—Minds would leave each other in contrary directions, traverse each other in Numberless points, and all [for at] last greet each other at the Journeys end—A old Man and a child would talk together and the old Man be led on his Path, and the child left thinking—[†]

2.

The Foot and the Leg

People observe their feet or write about them with a unique detachment. The foot is not quite a part of the rest of the body, not quite part of the mind and heart that direct actions and receive impressions. The foot is simply there, as the shoe that eventually may fit it is simply there.

Yet this does not mean that thoughts about the foot are simple or that people agree about its functions and, more provocatively, its character. Thoughts about the foot tend to exist in oppositions: the useful vs. the useless, the primitive or natural vs. the civilized, the animal vs. the spiritual, the physical vs. the mental, the heavy vs. the airy, the earthly vs. the spiritual, the ugly vs. the beautiful, the repulsive and disgusting vs. the sexually attractive and the adorable, the innocent vs. the seductive. The foot either responds to the body's commands or works from an independent center. The foot is a thing or it is human. Furthermore, the foot may stand metonymically for the body, for the whole person including the mind and will and desire, and for the walk. And, of course, it names the metrical unit of a line of poetry.

The foot mingles with the dust, lies in the mud, gets punctured by a nail, develops corns and callouses, smells badly of the day. But some wish to kiss another's foot. Some have been forced to wash the feet of those in power. The foot to some is base; to worship or serve it in some way demands the exhibition and admission of one's own baseness or "humility." One makes oneself low, as low as the foot, which rejects the humanly dignified posture of erectness. We, as Bataille says, are like a tree reaching upward. Indulging the foot, finding it seductive, signifies passional extravagance, fetishism, perversion.

On the other hand, the foot implies erectness and dignity. After all, it does not usually sink into the ground. It does not make us indistinguishable from earth but rather opposes the earth. The foot launches us forward and upward, at once platform and engine. "My foot is a border partaking of the double character of me and of the earth, a neutral zone separating me from the ground. . . . The footless, crippled beggars painted by Breughel are pathetic and disturbing chiefly because they have nothing between them and the earth. Without the foot do they qualify as human?"[†]

The foot has been subjected to Romantic analysis. The foot, says Alice Meynell, "has no longer a distinct and divided life, or any that is visible and sensible. Whereas the whole living body has naturally such infinite distinctness that the sense of touch differs, as it were, with every nerve, and the fingers are so separate that it was believed of them of old that each one had its angel, yet the modern foot is, as much as possible, deprived of all that delicate distinction: undone, unspecialized, sent back to lower forms of indiscriminate life."[†] Upon first reading this I imagined that this desire to restore to the foot a distinctness, to focus on the part rather than on the whole, was precisely counter to the Romantic understanding of modern society, the latter's tendency to separate person from person, part from part according to function, to alienate a limb from the animating center of the body. But Alice Meynell means the opposite. The distinctiveness of the foot must be envisioned "infinite," alive, weightless, a thing itself of play and imagination, not a limb but an organ its own animating center, giving its own directions, seeking and exploring with its own curiosity. She is talking not about the beautiful organizations and hierarchies of the body but, again metonymically, of the social misuse of power. Romantic liberty can be described with reference to the foot: when the foot is light, it draws the mind into it. A burden is lifted, which every walker knows, when the foot leads. When this liberty vanishes, writes seventeenth-century mystical poet Thomas Traherne, the foot turns to wood:

> To *walk* abroad is, not with eyes,
> But thoughts, the fields to see and prize;
> Else may the silent feet,
> Like logs of wood,
> Move up and down, and see no good,
> Nor joy nor glory meet.[†]

Romanticism, often perceiving attempts to control or limit the mind of the person as the great threat of modern life, sees the fate of liberty residing in mind itself. We cannot dream about a midnight murder any more, says William Hazlitt, because "the police spoils all."[†] For Blake the moment of mental freedom, raised to a visionary power, comes through the foot:

> And all this Vegetable World appeard on my left Foot,
> As a bright sandal formed immortal of precious stones & gold.
> I stooped down and bound it on to walk forward thro' Eternity.[†]

The foot of an infant lying on its back is wondrously weightless, useless; it is not an instrument for bearing that other thing, "the body." This foot tends upward and is like the antenna of an insect.

The leg negotiates the weight of the body. Achilles' feet, not his legs, are "swift"; Hermes' feet, not his legs, are winged. In Homer when the legs crumple from the spear shot, the body thunders to the dust.

Charles Lamb gushed over walking: "walked myself off my legs, dying walking!"[†] This would be life as a pleasurable fulfillment, a leavening of the body into spirit, the rhythm of the legs dissolving the weight of the legs into energy. "To walk one's legs off" does not indicate dismemberment. No violence hides beneath the swing of the legs. Along with the legs, one will have walked off self-consciousness, all heat. One may have arrived at what Rilke calls "the profound indifference of the heart."

Keats associated a growing skepticism about idealist values, a greater acceptance for the economic basis of human life and a questioning of its aesthetic basis, in short an increase in judgment and deliberation, with a change in the metaphor for human life—walking replaces flying:

THE WALK: NOTES ON A ROMANTIC IMAGE

I have of late been moulting: not for fresh feathers and wings: they are gone, and in their stead I hope to have a pair of patient sublunary legs . . . the very corn which is now so beautiful, as if it had only took to ripening yesterday, is for the market.[†]

Taken a step further, the limping leg emphasizes the sheer plod of the human person in the face of fantasy and wish but not so much as a defeat as a statement about human grittiness before reality. Freud, quoting Faust, says:

"Was man nicht erfliegen kann, muss man erhinken." What one cannot fly over, he must limp around.

Quoted more than once by Freud, this calls up the Freudian task, to replace or constrain fantasy by reality. Moving from flight to a limping gait appears to the grandiose mind as defeat but to the mind intent on accomplishment as victory. That such an exchange stirs up sinister feelings is evident in Freud's comparable though more awesome epigraph to *The Interpretation of Dreams*: Flectere si nequeo superos, Acheronta movebo: If I cannot move the heavens, I will move Hell.[†] The two passages were originally, I think, deep in the story of Hephaestos' fall from Olympus. When Zeus hurled his son Hephaestos from heaven for supporting Hera in a struggle with her husband, the king of Gods, the boy fell (buoyantly, beautifully) a long day to the Isle of Lemnos. The shock of landing produced the limp. Yet Homer knew vividly the recompense for the harsh defeat—the oedipal defeat. Appearing to be a good-natured bumbler serving nectar to the other gods provoked by his limp to laughter, Hephaestos asserts elsewhere his creative power as the maker of Achilles' vast shield and his sexual power as the lover of Aphrodite.

In introducing a portrait of his cousin, Charles Lamb indulges in some humility by contrasting his own writing to that of the masterful Sterne and the "pen of Yorick": "I must limp after in my poor antithetical manner, as the fates have given me grace and talent."[†] But sometimes, in order to acknowledge accurately the constraints of his art, the poet must resort to a more extravagant modification of upright mobility. Vergil picks up Dante as a mother picks up her child at a point where the walk through the Aquinian city of dreadful night becomes impossible. Legs are useless; they do not measure up to the visionary requirements of the moment. The temporary reversion to a childlike posture in the grasp of the mother-guide only makes him a walker with a more capacious visionary range. The legs intimate both the extent and the constraint of vision.

> I have two doctors, my left leg and my right. When body and mind are out of gear (and those twin parts of me live at such close quarters that the one always catches melancholy from the other) I know that I have only to call in my doctors and I shall be well again.[†]

Claiming that his legs were his doctors, George Macaulay Trevelyan makes the modern association of walking, sport, and health. The legs, burdened enough with the body they convey, must be further burdened with responsibility for that body's well-being!

Lying in bed one morning, Pablo Neruda watched his legs with the wonderment of a lover, adoring and dispassionate, the poet and phenomenologist and social critic all alive:

> Like stalks, like some winsome and feminine thing,
> they climb from my knees, compact and cylindrical,
> tight with the turbulent stuff of my life:
> brutish and lubberly, like the arms of a goddess,
> like trees monstrously clad in the guise of the human,
> like vast and malevolent lips, athirst and immobile,
> all the heft of my body waits there . . .
> And those legs, there, my masculine legs,
> unsensual, bluff, and resilient; endowed
> with their clustering muscles, complementary animals—
> they, too, are a life, a substantial and delicate world,
> alert and unfaltering, living watchful and strenuous there.

> So, to the ticklish extremes of my footsoles,
> stanch as the sun, and expanded like flowers,
> a troop in the wan wars of space, unflagging, resplendent—
> all come to an end, all that is living concludes in my feet:
> from there on, the hostile and alien begins:
> all the names of the world, outposts and frontiers,

THE WALK: NOTES ON A ROMANTIC IMAGE

the noun and its adjective that my heart never summoned
compact with consistency, cooly, emerge.[†]

The verb "to tread" refers either to the crushing, imprinting, plodding weight of the human body transmitted through the leg and foot, or it can refer to the opposite—a lightness or absence of weight, a footstep that refuses to transmit the human burden to the earth.

The word, moreover, has sexual roots. To Chaucer the words meant intercourse: Chauntecleer

> fethered Pertelote twenty tyme,
> And trad as ofte, er that it was pryme.[†]

Blake transforms this usage to his own apocalyptic sense, the violence of the sexual, creative, imagination: "O when shall we tread the wine-presses in heaven" or "How red the sons & daughters of Luvah how they tread the grapes."[†]

At times the treading foot signifies the weightlessness of dreams and the weightlessness of a foot, the caution and belief of a person who will not destroy dreams. Says Yeats in "He wishes for the Cloths of Heaven":

> Had I the heavens' embroidered cloths . . .
> I would spread the cloths under your feet:
> But I, being poor, have only my dreams;
> I have spread my dreams under your feet;
> Tread softly because you tread on my dreams."[†]

Dreams, suggests Milton, are like the spirit of nature:

> Whilst from off the waters fleet
> Thus I set my printless feet
> O'er the Cowslips Velvet head,
> That bends not as I tread.[†]

A goal of the Romantic poet is to capture in poetry the *genius loci*, or spirit of place. The airy tread that confounds physical reality leads the spirit to its sacred bower. The poet hopes for a innocent approach, but the tread means finally a stepping across the sacred boundary to spirit or dream, a transgression. Thus for Wordsworth and Keats the word "un-trodden" points to the most sacred space of all. "She dwelt among un-trodden ways" means that Lucy lived in a purity of being that ordinary lovers do not or cannot know, but the poet alludes to his knowledge of this fairest of all stars, this violet half-hidden from the eye. Did he tread *his* way to her? Are we to hear the Chaucerian overtone behind the elegiac seriousness? Keats reveals an Elizabethan, if not Chaucerian, eroticism in his "Ode to Psyche" when after treading his way through a forest and coming upon a vision of the pagan lovers Cupid and Psyche, he later exclaims:

> Yes, . . . build a fane
> In some untrodden region of my mind.[†]

Keats formulates the poetic act as a recovery of erotic spirit.

But this whole delicate affair could collapse, if not by a failure of that trickery and the illusion that the Romantic ideology banks on, then by the sheer plod of the foot. At times the weight of the foot pulls the human effort down toward the inert ground: "Generations have trod, have trod, have trod."[†] To the singing nightingale Keats exclaims: "No hungry generations tred thee down!"[†] Humankind burdened with the mystery or with the weary weight of the unintelligible world mechanically unloads its burden step by step for the duration of mortal days.

In Alberto Giacometti's famous *Homme qui marche* (bronze, 1960) there are, on those fearfully long legs, no knees. The source of power and desire and purposiveness for the modern person resides not—as it does for the Homeric warrior—in the knees but in the genital region.

In *Femme debout* (bronze, 1947) all parts of the woman's body sink, slide, push, melt together in a long stick, head and neck in particular sink between the shoulders and down into the torso. Breasts too hang down, barely visible along the belly. Fully upright, all her weight submits to gravity—nothing resists it. There is nothing but the vertical coordinate, no vectors of outward or forward drive or purpose. With the walker the energy of gravity in the woman is released, in a dramatic horizontal vector, toward the world. (In an odd way the skinny standing woman is an earth mother.) The shoulders free up the neck; the head moves forward behind the chin. The arms move back from the chest and grow tense at the elbows. The hands tense near the pelvis and groin, from which point the legs have suddenly moved apart from each other.

It is hard to see how this thin form propels itself lightly. If one thinks of muscles, body weight, normal proportions, it does not make sense.

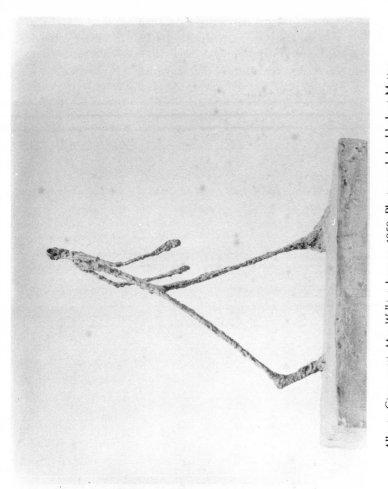

Alberto Giacometti, *Man Walking*, bronze, 1950 Photograph by Herbert Matter.

As an idea the sexual (genital) source of motion, the *desire* for it, is abstracted from the body's capacity to make it happen. Walking is the desire for life. For Giacometti "to walk" is an affirmative-intransitive verb, implying no object or destination, the manifestation of elemental human energy. That the walker comes in bronze adds to the walker's "elemental" nature. A person walking is as elemental as a person breathing or eating, a fact and principle of biology and mind.

3.

Throwing off the Burden

Walking and the Self

Unlike Giacometti's *Homme qui marche*, which reduces the walk to the elemental idea of human energy and desire, the Romantic walk is inevitably about "the self"—its coalescence or its liberation:

> For in this walk, this voyage,
> it is yourself, the profound history of your 'self,'
> that now as always you encounter.[†]

Hazlitt's excitement around the walk usually stems from this achievement:

> Give me the clear blue sky over my head, and the green turf beneath my feet, a winding road before me, and a three hours' march to dinner—and then to thinking! It is hard if I cannot start some game on these lone heaths. I laugh, I run, I leap, I sing for joy. From the point of yonder rolling cloud, I plunge into my past being, and revel there, as the sun-burnt Indian plunges headlong into the wave that wafts him to his native shore. Then long-forgotten things, like 'sunken wrack and sumless treasures,' burst upon my eager sight, and I begin to feel, think, and be myself again.[†]

What distinguishes William Hazlitt from typical English Romantic walkers is his pleasure in courting the primitive and passionate in himself, wherever they may lead. The walk brings the self into being by occasioning a flood from the forgotten, by bringing the past into the present. The classic essay from which this passage comes, "On Going a Journey" (1821), enacts the play and clash of past and present on Hazlitt's personal and political consciousness in one of the great, brief displays of critical Romantic experience. The release to the self given by the walk receives support from what actually are the constraints of nature: the "clear blue sky over my head, and the green turf beneath my feet, a winding road before me, and a three hours' march to dinner." What appears like an infinite release is really the Romantic illusion of infinity or openness. The three spatial dimensions and the temporal one give him plenty of space for his wandering but protect and limit him at the same time. This is the pastoral or idyllic context of Romantic walking. Most Romantic writers stay within it, but Hazlitt's critical politics, his refusal of cultural complacency, makes him a restless walker and a restless man. Indeed, Robert L. Stevenson—whose "Walking Tours" acknowledges the debt to Hazlitt's essay by declaring it "so good that there should be a tax levied on all who have not read it"—still complains of Hazlitt-as-walker:

> I do not approve of that leaping and running. Both of these hurry the respiration; they both shake up the brain out of its glorious open-air confusion; and they both break the pace. Uneven walking is not so agreeable to the body, and it distracts and irritates the mind. Whereas, when once you have fallen into an equable stride, it requires no conscious thought from you to keep it up, and yet it prevents you from thinking earnestly of anything else. Like knitting, like the work of a copying clerk, it gradually neutralises and sets to sleep the serious activity of the mind.[†]

This Hazlitt is never willing to do. His self, revealed in the walk, continues the private/public labor of trying to make sense of himself as a walker through English society and history.

To go a journey is to throw off a burden, what Wordsworth called at the beginning of *The Prelude*:

> That burthen of my own unnatural self,
> The heavy weight of many a weary day
> Not mine, and such as were not made for me.[†]

Psychologically many walkers know both this desire and the experience of unburdening themselves on the walk. But Wordsworth puts it in a special way that has a social implication beyond the notation of the good feelings that the walk brings. The rest of this opening passage announces the joy not simply of walking but of leaving the city, the site and cause of that burden, the snatcher of days. To recover the self (to "be myself again") means to leave society and history and return to nature free as a bird:

> O welcome messenger! O welcome friend!
> A captive greets thee, coming from a house
> Of bondage, from yon city's walls set free,
> A prison where he hath been long immured.
> Now I am free, enfranchis'd and at large,
> May fix my habitation where I will.
> What dwelling shall receive me? In what Vale
> Shall be my harbour? Underneath what grove
> Shall I take up my home, and what sweet stream
> Shall with its murmurs lull me to my rest?
> The earth is all before me: with a heart
> Joyous, not scar'd at its own liberty,
> I look about, and should the guide I chuse
> Be nothing better than a wandering cloud,
> I cannot miss my way.†

Burdened, imprisoned, disenfranchised, the walker enters the walk to return home. Nature, he anticipates, will provide that home. Alone, he nonetheless moves in a world of friendliness. The same is true of Walt Whitman in "Song of the Open Road":

> Afoot and light-hearted I take to the open road,
> Healthy, free, the world before me,
> The long brown path before me leading wherever I choose.
>
> Henceforth I ask not good-fortune, I myself am good-fortune,
> Henceforth I whimper no more, postpone no more, need nothing,
> Done with indoor complaints, libraries, querulous criticisms,
> Strong and content I travel the open road.
>
> The earth, that is sufficient,
> I do not want the constellations any nearer,

I know they are very well where they are,
I know they suffice for those who belong to them.

(Still here I carry my old delicious burdens,
I carry them, men and women, I carry them with me wherever I go,
I swear it is impossible for me to get rid of them,
I am fill'd with them; and I will fill them in return.)[†]

Full of joy, anticipation, strength, the wish to announce their plan
and good fortune, Wordsworth and Whitman nonetheless model themselves upon Milton's Adam and Eve leaving Paradise—a sorrowful exit
and beginning:

The World was all before them, where to choose
Thir place of rest, and Providence thir guide:
They hand in hand with wandring steps and slow
Through Eden took thir solitary way.[†]

The Wordsworthian walk reverses the direction of the Miltonic one:
Adam and Eve head toward history and the world's future cities; Wordsworth leaves urban civilization and history for the supposed timelessness
of nature. Their journey marks their error (to wander is to "err"). Wordsworth's and Whitman's journey declares their present freedom from error
or sin, the correctness of their choice. Burdens for Wordsworth come
from the failures of nourishment in city life. They are inner struggle,
psychological disease. For Milton burden is sin, the consequence of er-
rant passion, the walk from Eden manifesting that moral errancy in history. Choice for Adam and Eve only prevails within the severe limits of
Providence and measures at once their dignity but also the apparent
chaos and darkness of history upon which they enter. The Romantics
walk out of choice (or claim to)—according to them a good choice.
The walk gives them abundance, but for Adam and Eve, Edenic abundance fades the further away from Eden they walk.

The three walks to which I have just referred are all on the epic scale.
Although you or I may simply arise from our seat for a morning or evening walk from which we later return to resume a habitual life, the epic
walker's walk signals a momentous change of state, a shift in the organization of the civilized world, an action taken against it. Kafka, who
could write epic on the smallest scale, recounts "A Sudden Walk" in the
setting of domestic family politics:

THE WALK: NOTES ON A ROMANTIC IMAGE

When it looks as if you had made up your mind finally to stay at home for the evening, when you have put on your house jacket and sat down after supper with a light on the table to the piece of work or the game that usually precedes your going to bed, when the weather outside is unpleasant so that staying indoors seems natural, and when you have already been sitting quietly at the table for so long that your departure must occasion surprise to everyone, when, besides, the stairs are all in darkness and the front door locked, and in spite of all that you have started up in a sudden fit of restlessness, changed your jacket, abruptly dressed yourself for the street, explained that you must go out and with a few curt words of leave-taking actually gone out, banging the flat door more or less hastily according to the degree of displeasure you think you have left behind you, and when you find yourself once more in the street with limbs swinging extra freely in answer to the unexpected liberty you have procured for them, when as a result of this decisive action you feel concentrated within yourself all the potentialities of decisive action, when you recognize with more than usual significance that your strength is greater than your need to accomplish effortlessly the swiftest of changes and to cope with it, when in this frame of mind you go striding down the long streets— then for that evening you have completely got away from your family, which fades into insubstantiality, while you yourself, a firm, boldly drawn black figure, slapping yourself on the thigh, grow to your true stature.

All this is still heightened if at such a late hour in the evening your look up a friend to see how he is getting on.[†]

The background for this walk and the occasion for its suddenness and violence is ordinary, habitual domesticity—on the surface peaceful and comforting in its peacefulness but apparently masking a terrible rigidity or tenseness. From one point of view the walk is an uprooting, from another a rejection and dismissal of the family, and from a third a release: Kafka feels it all three ways though the last way prevails. The reader, bound to the walker at every step, learns the meaning of the previous step at about the same time the walker does. What was implicit in the heat of action becomes explicit with the walker's distance from the house. Only toward the end of the paragraph does the reader or the walker realize fully that the newfound stature coincided with distance from an oppressive family that stands for and dispenses the rigidities of a relentlessly dull domestic order. Not only do the new energy and growth come as victory over the family but they signal the affiliative direction this energy will take.

For a walker, interiors may not so much cultivate as stifle freedom of mind. (How many writers, thinkers, artists, scientists, politicians demand of themselves the walk?) Kafka's sudden walk leads us to think that a pressure for unconstrained mental activity was building within him, perhaps coming on precisely because of or in response to the sheer fact of an oppressive situation. A paradox of the walker's fantasy and experience is that as one enters the variety and movement of the outside world, the space for interior wandering also grows. In nature this is not surprising, but the city walker, like Kafka, encounters the same inner landscape as he treads the paths of civic intercourse. What the rural and urban walkers may dream will usually be different, however. Buildings and streets cause different kinds of internal activity than do fields and birds and streams. But for Wordsworth the placid surface of a lake, mirroring heaven, calms the walker's mind into strength.

De Quincey said that Wordsworth probably walked a hundred thousand miles. The poet's legs served him remarkably well for eight decades. At Wordsworth's final home of thirty-seven years, Rydal Mount, the visitor can see the path, designed by the poet, leading from the main house to a tiny roofed shelter thirty-or-so yards away, a straight path for walking and composing up and down the earth. At the far end of Grasmere by the base of Helm Crag the poet of *The Prelude* composed while walking to and fro. Near these poetic walking places are the two lakes, Rydal Mere and Grasmere respectively. Dorothy Wordsworth writes best and briefly about Grasmere:

> Grasmere looked so beautiful that my heart was almost melted away. It was quite calm, only spotted with sparkles of light.[†]

> The air was become still the lake was of a bright slate colour, the hills darkening.

> It is a breathless grey day that leaves the golden woods of autumn quite in their own tranquillity, stately and beautiful in their decaying, the lake is a perfect mirror.[†]

My own preference is for Rydal Mere with its soft shoreline of reeds that make the line between lake and land nearly a thing of the imagination.

Glimpsed in snatches through the thick foliage down from the Rydal Mount lawn, it is made dazzling white by a strong sun, almost invisible under the low clouds.

Although he writes little about walking around these lakes, Wordsworth clearly established his need for them and knew his pleasure with them. At least three times he writes memorably about the meaning of the lake for the walker. In his story of the leech gatherer, *Resolution and Independence*, he, "a traveller upon the moors," encounters the ancient man "Beside a pool bare to the eye of heaven." The leech gatherer, forever stirring the pool with his stick, seems beyond time, "feet and head Coming together in life's pilgrimage." The walker's restoration of himself comes about by the convergence of his own "untoward thoughts" with the old man by his heavenly pool.[†]

Restoration is the object of the poet's lake walks upon returning home from college:

> Those walks did now like a returning spring
> Come back on me again. When first I made
> Once more the circuit of our little lake
> If ever happiness hath lodged with man
> That day consummate happiness was mine—
> Wide-spreading, steady, calm, contemplative.
> The sun was set, or setting, when I left
> Our cottage door, and evening soon brought on
> A sober hour, not winning or serene,
> For cold and raw the air was, and untuned;
> But as a face we love is sweetest then
> When sorrow damps it, or, whatever look
> It chance to wear, is sweetest if the heart
> Have fulness in itself, even so with me
> It fared that evening. Gently did my soul
> Put off her veil, and, self-transmuted, stood
> Naked as in the presence of her God.
> As on I walked, a comfort seemed to touch
> A heart that had not been disconsolate,
> Strength came where weakness was not known to be,
> At least not felt; and restoration came
> Like an intruder knocking at the door
> Of unacknowledged weariness.[†]

Is it the lake that raises to a higher power the contentment granted the walker? *The Prelude* tells the story of one for whom "feeling comes in aid of feeling," happiness redounds to earlier happinesses, the comedy of inner fulness confirms itself by earlier comedies. The mind becomes the lake (wide-spreading, steady, calm) that the body circumambulates. The lake becomes the "contemplative" mind. The intruder, the foreign invasive force, converts to the opposite: comfort and restoration.

Wordsworth's lake derives from Rousseau's lake of Bienne. Rousseau did not walk around it but floated on it. He records as a supremely elemental restorative sensation the rocking motion of his boat. Wordsworth is at one remove, walking. The exquisite lyric "Stepping Westward" hints that the encounter with the lake is supposed to heal a walker's loneliness:

> 'What, you are stepping westward?'—'Yea.'
> —'Twould be a *wildish* destiny,
> If we, who thus together roam
> In a strange Land, and far from home,
> Were in this place the guests of Chance:
> Yet who would stop, or fear to advance,
> Though home or shelter he had none,
> With such a sky to lead him on?
>
> The dewy ground was dark and cold;
> Behind, all gloomy to behold;
> And stepping westward seemed to be
> A kind of *heavenly* destiny:
> I like the greeting; 'twas a sound
> Of something without place or bound;
> And seemed to give me spiritual right
> To travel through that region bright.
>
> The voice was soft, and she who spake
> Was walking by her native lake:
> The salutation had to me
> The very sound of courtesy:
> Its power was felt; and while my eye
> Was fixed upon the glowing Sky,
> The echo of the voice enwrought
> A human sweetness with the thought

Of travelling through the world that lay
Before me in my endless way.[†]

A book could be written on Wordsworth as a walker. For more than half-a-century of his poetry the walk characterizes his entry into experience. One would expect his walking poetry to reveal a comfort about walking. Yet that anticipated comfort belongs more to a vision of possibility than to the actuality. His early walkers are not himself but characters (in *Salisbury Plain* and *The Borderers*) who walk out of their social alienation: outlaws, murderers, people stung to the core with guilt, the dispossessed and disenfranchised, abandoned women, discharged soldiers, beggars and gypsies. The poet identifies with such figures, first as people rejected by society and the ruling classes and secondly and at least as problematically burdened with his conviction of his own severe family losses. Wordsworth here caught from Rousseau, also parentless growing up, the walk as a dream of restoration and early bonding and like Rousseau has wedded that dream to the ideology of the "essential" person defined libidinally by his *amour de soi*. No poem by Wordsworth alludes more compactly and austerely to the poet's mournful base of emptiness and the energy for his vision of fullness than "Stepping Westward."

The woman in "Stepping Westward" instills trust in the walker as he enters the unknown. She is Wordsworth's version of the protective female figure in myth and literature assuring and guiding the hero on his journey: an Ariadne, a Beatrice. Such a protectress evokes feelings of maternal trust but also anticipates the civilized world to which she provides a bridge. The speaker observes that the woman is walking by her native lake but is also struck by her words and voice, which, with its "sound of courtesy," suggests the civilized world.

More than this, the woman's greeting and her recollection of it spiritualizes the world. Let me list the verbal conversions or sublimations. The pronoun changes from "we" to "I"; and the "destiny" from "wildish," uncertain gothic, to "heavenly," serene, consoling. The phrase, "What, you are stepping westward?" means not as language but as "sound": the sound is "soft," and "Its power was *felt*." The effect of the phrase and of these displacements of language is finally synthesized in the last four lines of the poem, where the *echo* and not the voice acts to comfort the walker, and the echo produces a "human sweetness."

Throughout the poem the eye fixes upon a sky growing more substantial than the earth upon which he walks. The sky, not the woman or the ground, is "glowing." By contrast, the earth is forbidding and strangely insubstantial, like a clammy sepulchre or the Vergilian underworld through which Aeneas walks, with its "inane" darkness. In stanza two the poet focuses on the ground only to make more vivid the "heavenly" orientation of the woman's phrase, "a sound Of something without place or bound." The sky develops some of the comforting permanence of heaven itself. The phrase "stepping westward" catches some of the religious intent of Donne's "riding westward" toward Christ with the paradoxical sense of comfort and adventure, of leaving the world to find a home in spirit. Similarly, in "the world that lay Before me" one hears the fate of Milton's walkers: "the world was all before them." But "the world" for Adam and Eve—the place of the fall, death, sexuality, self-consciousness, and history itself—has in "Stepping Westward" been passed by, in the idyllic hope of a spiritual walk. The phrase "human sweetness" is reminiscent of what Dante the walker knows in *Paradiso*, XXXIII. For him, paradoxically, the senses carry the permanence of the now-faded and complete vision of eternity. For Wordsworth the reduction of vision, or language, to sweetness does not imply the Dantean or Miltonic grappling with history and self. Divinity has not overwhelmed or beckoned to itself a worldly, passionate man. At the end of Canto XXXIII "desire and will" yield to the power of divine love. The driving energies of self are subjected to a greater impulse and not in themselves diminished. But in "Stepping Westward" world, ground, desire, and will dissolve or weaken. The self that emerges is only validated as "spirit" in a heavenly geography of an "endless way."

Denise Levertov wrote a "Stepping Westward" poem that may represent the antiphonal, unspoken thoughts of Wordsworth's woman. The native lake, of origins and destinations, that compensation for emptiness and alienation, disappears. The woman revels in her unconcern about beginnings and endings; she defines herself confidently and pleasurably in motion, responsive to nature, fully human, and perhaps as defiant as she is natural:

> . . . a shadow
> that grows longer as the sun
> moves, drawn out

on a thread of wonder.
If I bear burdens

they begin to be remembered
as gifts, goods, a basket

of bread that hurts
my shoulders but closes me

in fragrance. I can
eat as I go.[†]

"I wandered lonely as a cloud / That floats on high o'er vales and hills."[†] A walk without substance, a walk before consciousness begins and before the earth and the body begin. "Lonely" is the only human reference, as if spirit could somehow be isolated before it enters human life. The poem is not simply about an event that lives in imagination. Rather it describes the onset of the passions. Seeing the daffodils, the walker comes down to earth and erotic sensibility. Wandering lonely as a cloud is wandering formlessly, without boundary; it is passiveness and not wise passiveness. He is an object for meteorologists . . . and all object. The vales and hills are nothing but landscape. They could have been the female body, but that would have necessitated the walker's subjectivity and his accessibility to his own passions. The walker, say the psychoanalysts, *transgresses* the body of the earth, usurping what does not rightfully belong to him. But this walker—an inert phenomenon of nature and poetry—transgresses nothing. Put more positively, he is like Schiller's developmental stage called "filled infinity," which must resolve into boundary and limit to become real, vivid.

Valery sets the following proportion: poetry is to prose as the dance is to the walk. For him the walk is strict utility. It sets the shortest distance. The walker has a goal not himself, and therefore the walk does not reverberate in the achievement but dissolves into it:

When this man has completed his movement, when he has reached the place, the book, the fruit, the object he desired, this possession immediately annuls his whole act, the effect consumes the cause, the end absorbs the means, and whatever the modalities of his act and steps, only the result remains.[†]

Prose similarly vanishes after it has uttered its communication. Dancing (poetry) is different: "It goes nowhere. Or if it pursues anything it is only an ideal object, a delight, the phantom of a plower, or some transport out of oneself, an extreme of life, a summit, a supreme point of being."† Applying Valery to Wordsworth, I find that walking and the prose had disappeared before the dancing (and poetry) began. Or rather, the walking and prose had issued into dancing and poetry, and the burden had lifted.

THE WALK: NOTES ON A ROMANTIC IMAGE

4.

The Walking Essay and the Compulsion to Collect

For no subgenre of literature do Virginia Woolf's remarks on the requirements for the essay—that it "lap us about and draw its curtain across the world"†—apply more aptly than for the walking essay. If one does not, at least while reading such an essay, believe in the cozy pleasure of essay reading, a pleasure in which the mind is active but refuses the sharp twists and turns of mind in its most elaborate purposefulness, then one should not waste time with walking essays. In the walking essay familiarity is its own solution; it confirms itself. One walks either to make a destination, or one walks for the pleasure of walking, says the walking tradition. If you choose the latter walk, you approximate the choice to read a walking essay. I myself discovered the walking essay a few minutes after being a tourist at Salisbury Cathedral. Walking back from the cathedral grounds into the town, I went into a bookstore where, after circling around the dusty shelves, I came upon *The Lore of the Wanderer: An Open-Air Anthology*, edited by George Goodchild. This book, with a dull purple binding and just the right size for a well-seamed back pocket and with two strangely coy angels on the inside cover, gave me forever Hazlitt's "On Going a Journey," R. L. Stevenson's "Walking Tours," and Dickens's "Night Walks." From this modest beginning I have since discovered that the world of the last two centuries has spawned many such pieces, that walkers, who are almost always bona fide essayists, are urged from somewhere to ambulate on paper about ambulation.

Yet part of the pleasure of walking essays is simply thinking *about* them, knowing that they exist, collecting in one's mind all these little byways into familiarity. There are indications that the essayists themselves indulged the same pleasure, for they sometimes quote one of their predecessors approvingly or assert that they carry a copy of Hazlitt's "On Going a Journey" on every hike. The compulsion to collect is in fact related to the compulsion to repeat, which in turn generates the longing to make one's own version of the same thing. Finally one must admit that the pleasures of reading, collecting, and even writing walking essays are basically oral: is it any wonder that the climax of several of them (Hazlitt, Stevenson, Stephens) is the stop at the inn for dinner, or the arrival at the top of the mountain, which occasions the unpacking of sandwiches or the lighting up one's favorite pipe? Nor are we surprised when we see Thoreau ("with relish," as Hazlitt would say) open Vergil and Wordsworth in his tent or when we discover that Aldous Huxley devoted an entire essay to "Books for the Journey." According to George Macaulay Trevelyan the longer one walks, the closer one approximates a "natural" state of simple desires and full health. Nothing could satisfy more than three boiled eggs, strong tea, and a basic anthology of English poems or French aphorisms.

I have not encountered an essay more calculated to satisfy the most basic needs of one "hungry" for essayistic nourishment—indeed, essays like the following one might compare to the pleasure of wine, cheese, and French bread in the mountains—than E. V. Lucas's "A Journey Round a Room." It can be found in a volume of his essays called *Turning Things Over* (1929). Let us suppose for the moment that "turning things over" itself constitutes a basic pleasure: engaging in successions of events, scenes, objects, or leafing through a book. Some poets of the nineteenth century—Wordsworth, Coleridge, Keats, Hugo, Baudelaire—at times referred to these successions of images that they cultivated and often described as reveries or waking dreams, in which a thing would appear before one luminous and real, though never real in permanence or touch, and then would be turned over and replaced by another thing, the previous one having disappeared from sight and become unavailable to memory. Part of the pleasure of reverie surely includes the absence of memory. There can be no longing, no gap between any unfulfillment of the moment and some fulfillment in the past. If longing enters one's house of experience, then reverie in its purest and most desirable form is no longer operative. Virginia Woolf speaks of the ideal essay in terms of its power to lure one into, and keep one in, a waking dream. The essay

> should lay us under a spell with its first word, and we should only wake, re-freshed, with its last. In the interval we may pass through the most various experiences of amusement, surprise, interest, indignation; we may soar to the heights of fantasy with Lamb or plunge to the depths of wisdom with Bacon, but we must never be roused. The essay must lap us about and draw its curtain across the world.[†]

Turning Things Over, then, is a fine title for a book of essays, one of which is "A Journey Round a Room." From this essay and the mild rev-erie we drop into when we give our sympathies to Lucas, we are never roused. Those basic appetites of the reader of essays, "locomotion" and collection or, more viscerally, hoarding, are here satisfied. "A Journey Round a Room" has been given a narrative frame: left alone for two hours in the house of some friends who were suddenly called away, Lucas decided to entertain himself by describing what was in the room. He says he was inspired in this direction by an eighteenth-century soldier-author, Xavier de Maistre, who, "as a punishment for his share in a forbidden duel at Turin, when serving with the Piedmontese army, was confined to his lodging for some weeks, and, being bored, filled up the time by writing a description of its contents, with all the digres-sions—some of them not ungallant—to which they gave rise."[†] Two prerequisites for this activity appear to be confinement and the immi-nent possibility of boredom. The nineteenth century has many ex-amples of the freedom and pleasure of the mind as a chosen conse-quence to physical imprisonment. Indeed in the cases of Leigh Hunt painting his prison cell to look like nature and Julien Sorel at the end of *The Red and the Black* achieving some inner peace in his cell, the topos becomes a political statement on the capacity of the human spirit to transcend the confinement of the body and therefore is a statement on the ineffectiveness of such a mode of punishment. The prison has be-come the "happy prison." Necessity, the necessity of avoiding boredom or worse, is the mother of this kind of essay. Out of boredom the essayist goes on a journey, however modest, out of boredom and into pleasure. Lucas makes it clear, however, that there have been for him two journeys: the first around the room and the second on the pieces of paper on which days later he wrote down his recollection of the first. The technique of this second journey was dedicated to simplicity in form and leisure in its execution. In the room was a dazzling array of pictures and *objects d'art*, which created, as Keats said, "a wide wandering for the greediest eye." Lucas simply described one, and another, and another, stepping from one to the next. The structure of the essay, paragraph to paragraph, followed the pictures and objects around the room, with indulgences in, for example, the biography of the artist or owner or personal anecdotes to fill out the paragraphs. For example:

> Among the silver in which this room was rich the best piece was a teapot by one of the few women silversmiths, Hester Bateman, whose work, whether in teapots, milk-jugs, or sugar-basins, has a peculiar gentle charm. Our most distinguished painter of still life, Mr. William Nicholson, is devoted to Hester, and you will find her creations lovingly depicted on many of his canvases. I can find out very little about her, except that she flourished at the end of the eighteenth century and took to the craft because her husband became blind. I should like to know more.
>
> After silver, brass. On nails on a panel hung several of those shining clanking ornaments which, as they swing, make the approach of a team of cart-horses so musical and cheerful, and which the zealous waggoner polishes with such pride. Some people collect them, and I saw not long ago a number of them at the Old Bell at Hurley—an inn which always brings to my mind the reply of an Italian waiter there when I asked him how he liked our English Thames, which flows a few steps away. He could not say, he said, because he had not yet walked so far! Perhaps the best way in which I can explain this particular harness ornament is to quote a passage from a letter which I received a little time since. 'Old G. was buried to-day, another link gone. They took him in his own waggon and favorite horses. He always wanted to be taken with Vi'let and Rebel, but they both died before he did, so it had to be Jule, Vi'let's daughter, a gay young filly of fifteen or sixteen summers. His own daughters have nursed him for four years, and haven't really had a night's unbroken rest all that time. Just imagine it, and I get so grumpy if I have one bad night!' Old G. was a Sussex farmer whom I first knew forty-four years

ago, and he struck me as an oldish man then, with his coarse yellow bushy beard and his blue eyes and a slow and not unsuspicious—at any rate, very cautious—manner of speech. His boots were always caked with clay from his heavy wealden land, out of which he himself seemed to have grown quite as much as his wheat or mangolds.[†]

This walking essay fulfills the desire for turning things over, for the experience of "life" as the nineteenth century often says it—as a sequence (rather than a conglomerate) of encounters while it satisfied the hunger for collecting, for hoarding and acquiring. Every event turned over in the journey of the essay remains on the page without loss from view, a perpetual reverie, a largely nonelegiac literary form. Acquisition seems to be an important impulse behind the familiar essayist's activity. Essayists love to list things, particularly, though not by any means exclusively, books. As many essays as there are about walking, there are perhaps twice as many or more about book collections, libraries, books-I-have-enjoyed. Here, perhaps, the impulse is the collection of the important symbolic artifacts of one's civilization, the creation of a kind of city of symbols. Is there not, finally, a connection between an account of a journey round a room through a private library and Vergil's or Dante's accounts of their journeys through the underworld? Each poet "acquires" the images of civilization for himself and for his age through the "walk" that each hero takes. From this point of view the hero, Aeneas or Dante, becomes a stylistic as well as perspectival orderer of meaning and image, and each serves his author's desire to acquire what he could get in no other way. "Writers," says Walter Benjamin in "Unpacking My Library," "are really people who write books not because they are poor, but because they are dissatisfied with the books which they could buy but do not like.[†]

To be sure, one must be, as Benjamin says, a bit whimsical when discussing book collecting and, I would add, walking essays. It is whimsy that allows one to tolerate comparisons between Vergil and E. V. Lucas. And it is whimsy that produces the "theories" of book collecting of Joyce Kilmer and A. A. Milne. Having just recently unpacked his library, A. A. Milne had not found time, or better, had refused to find time, to order the books properly, systematically:

To come to Keats is no guarantee that we are on the road to Shelley. Shelley, if he did not drop out on the way, is probably next to *How to be a Golfer though Middle-aged*.

Having written as far as this, I had to get up and see where Shelley really was. It is worse than I thought. He is between *Geometrical Optics* and *Studies in New Zealand Scenery*. Ella Wheeler Wilcox, whom I find myself to be entertaining unawares, sits beside *Anarchy or Order*, which was apparently "sent in the hope that you will become a member of the Duty and Discipline Movement"—a vain hope, it would seem, for I have not yet paid my subscription. *What I found Out*, by an English Governess, shares a corner with *The Recreations of a Country Parson*; they are followed by *Villette* and *Baedeker's Switzerland*. Something will have to be done about it.[†]

Kilmer praises the "inefficient library" as opposed to the public, or efficient one, a library dedicated to order and usefulness. In both of these essays the emphasis is on values that are only peripherally related to the specific passion designed for a specific book. This intellectual focus, emphasized by the efficient library, denies the love that can exist between a book and its owner, the purely aesthetic and sentimental considerations such as binding, illustrations, editorial features, previous owners, circumstances of purchase, etc. Here again is Benjamin:

> Thus there is in the life of a collector a dialectical tension between the poles of order and disorder. Naturally, his existence is tied to many other things as well: to a very mysterious relationship to ownership . . . also, to a relationship to objects which does not emphasize their functional, utilitarian value—that is, their usefulness—but studies and loves them as the scene, the stage, of their fate. The most profound enchantment for the collector is the locking of individual items within a magic circle in which they are fixed as the final thrill, the thrill of acquisition, passes over them. Everything remembered and thought, everything conscious, becomes the pedestal, the frame, the base, the lock of his property.[†]

The essay-as-collection is not too different because it fixes in a relatively ordered permanence an individual's desire to find the events and observations of his life meaningful and pleasurable even if, as is sometimes the case in brief familiar essays, the events and observations are trivial in themselves.

THE WALK: NOTES ON A ROMANTIC IMAGE

5.

Autobiographical Reflections

Walking, Romanticism, Criticism

I.

When I was five years old my family took a vacation in Steamboat Springs, Colorado. One morning I stepped alone out of our cabin and walked purposively down a dirt path crossing a sagebrush mesa. The earth was all before me, the mountains were around me, and childhood energy was propelling me. Suddenly, with a great hiss from a dusty bush against the path, a fat snake shot across my way, stretching itself forbiddingly. My terror was so general and primitive that, in memory at least, I became all legs and mouth as I ran home, or to where I thought home was, hoping to leave behind me the sullen, fanged road. That night I dreamt of a clear pond into which were thrown horsehairs that then muscled into poisonous snakes and back again into horsehairs. I had lost trust in the ground.

I do not think it too extravagant to date my attraction to Romanticism from this traumatic event. Surely my (ambivalent) attraction to the figure of the walk must date from it. For what is a walk if not an assertion of one's faith in the firmness of the earth and in the pleasure of one's foot meeting the ground? Or, if one is not capable of such an assertion, if one is bearing a trauma like the one just described, one may wish to try out the earth, to test it for its solidity, to grant one's feet some confidence, one's mind some freedom.

35

Jules Renard: "Walks. The body advances, while the mind flutters around it like a bird."[†]

Louis Aragon: "New myths are born beneath each of our steps."[†]

Jules Renard's civilizing walk, with its faith in a space for mind and body, a cooling current—what James Wright called

> . . . this cave
> In the air behind my body
> That nobody is going to touch.[†]

requires that I recognize the opposite, the walk that seems to invite an intrusion or invasion of what could be death itself. The protective and invigorating space does not resist the strike of the serpent. The current vanishes with the sudden rustle in the grass and hiss on the road. No one has recorded this invasion better than Homer in this simile of marshall fear and self-dissolution:

> As a man who has come on a snake in the mountain valley
> suddenly steps back, and the shiver comes over his body,
> and he draws back and away, cheeks seized with a green pallor;
> so in terror of Atreus' son godlike Alexandros
> lost himself again in the host of the haughty Trojans.[†]

Inverting the parts of the simile, one concludes that the encounter with the menacing reptile not only precipitates a loss of trust in the ground but that it reveals that the walk has prevailed upon the walker to assume a position—which the snake subverts—of domination, of power.

Twice I have not seen but only heard the menace, once while crossing a vacant lot behind my house in Denver, when it hissed beneath the weeds, and again while walking along a country road in Amenia, New York. That I might have startled or frightened *it* never occurred to me. I am the innocent, and it has lurked in the brush for my approach. Once, at age twelve, walking along a road to a beach on Cape Cod, the distance a blur because I had left my glasses at home, I suddenly noticed a coiled lump at the side of the road and imagined its head wiggling and poking in my direction. The seven years that separated me from Steamboat Springs dropped away and I ran back up the road to our house in complete terror.

I used to dream of snakes encountered on walks. The strangest snake chased me through the woods, rolling, like a runaway wheel, after me with its tail in its mouth—hostile yet (perhaps?) creative. Once in a dream a huge snake appeared before a chariot I was driving. The chariot crushed it, but far off in the weeds was a tiny snake, deadly poisonous and unseen.

City walks bring different terrors, for example, the terror of invasion by the insane. On a winter evening in downtown Denver—a city where one is continually surprised by how few people walk its expensive downtown streets—after the rush hour had passed, I waited alone for a bus. A man who must have thought he was a graceful bird flew over the street (his mittens flopping from his wrists) in the midst of the quiet. The silence and the isolatedness (in the city one gravitates to the swarm of walkers) caused the shock and the fear when this deranged, unbuoyed figure circled near me. I pretended that he was not there.

Once, as a young adolescent, trying on a new sense of freedom, I was walking with a gang of friends miles from home in an unknown part of Denver:

> Four of us, twelve years
> apiece, walked homeward from town,
> in tenuous new skins of
> freedom.
> A casual grey
> gloom of another, hostile
> unit of four twelve-year olds
> filled up the path before us
> anxious to fight. The meeting
> was pure in the violence
> of feeling. Hatred trickled
> down unhindered among us,
> and stunned us. Fear too loomed up,
> but this could not be expressed
> in our bleak new brotherhood.
> I watched on, desperately
> cultivating, invoking
> a god of anonymity,
> a new god, one I had not

imagined lived and whom even
now I wish I could murder.
But he bowed smiling in grey
and made me invisible
while one of them hit one of
us on the cheek with his fist.
He flushed, winced, but was not hurt,
the blow a gesture of hate,
a light brushstroke of malice.
My core seemed forever bruised:
How to regain my body
or stride into a new one?
But the groups detached and fell
away. We walked home over
tracks and bridges, sullen but
intact.

II.

The walking poet Reg Saner recently declared to me with conviction: "the walk is in the rhythm. It is . . . cosmic." As I climbed beyond Guanella Pass, the space around my body grew. I realized that I had let the space around me, in Denver, become all angles and walls cutting me off not from the outside world of the city but from my continuity with the world. (This is a suburban, not an urban, problem.) Beyond Guanella Pass the body does not protect itself from what is not itself. The body is on a *gradient* with the natural world; it *gradually* leaves its prison and its separateness as I walk along the *grade*. (L. *gradus*, step)

The recreation of the walk in prose or poetry weds that gradient of body and natural world to the self-as-mind-and-desire.

When recurring to my own past as a walker, not only the snake episode is indelible. I remember that even before that trauma I walked in the smiling country of Dutchess County, New York, with grandfathers. To walk along a winding dirt driveway following a line of towering horse chestnut trees and crossing a deep field in front of a pre–Revolutionary War house and clasping an old strong hand seemed the definition of friendship. The soft, regular sounds of the old man's steps went un-

THE WALK: NOTES ON A ROMANTIC IMAGE

noticed, and the skip of the very young child sent up puffs of fine dust in the path.

Today I usually walk alone but know that I am not alone on my "endless way." For there is a distance, from the beginning, on a walk when I am convinced of friendship, when it is all around. The two women in "Stepping Westward" speak friendship to the poet with their cry— "What? You are stepping westward?"—not because of the content of the words but because they reach him at an advanced moment in his walking. One must have traveled far enough to disengage the process of getting started, so that the welcoming of a greeting (it does not have to emanate from a human source) has nothing to do with the encumbrance of the effort to accept the solitude of one's walking. This friendship comes from an already established lightness of step.

How, further, does walking evoke the sense of friendship? When my mind breaks free into its own pleasure, it fastens onto my central preoccupations—usually obsessions or goals and plans. I prefer the obsession since, by definition, it will not vanish: I have to do nothing special to keep it in place. My mind simply works out and around it but is held in orbit by the tether of the obsession itself.

An obsession has a strong element of discomfort. Sometimes thinking while sitting or lying down can be painful if ideas and images flood the mind. Sometimes I lose my control over them through the vertigo of profusion. I even want to sleep, to deny thinking altogether. But thinking walking seems to grant physical space to the ideas that no longer crowd or huddle like sheep trying to squeeze through a small gate all at once. There is now room not only for associations but even for dialogue.

In rare thinking walking, dialogue replaces negation. One does not exclude an idea but can test or challenge it. The sense of friendship comes when some idea can announce itself, parade and show itself with no fear of being squelched by the profusion of images or by the self's warning against its own grandiosity. At such times one's thinking, like the body on the walk but more slowly, takes a step forward.

Romanticism has made walking an idyllic pastime. The walking essay—by and large a nineteenth- and twentieth-century response to a fear of the industrial city—has reinforced this assumption that the walk is an idyll that produces an inconsequential reverie. But the walk can go beyond the idyll since I can step forward in thought. Rigidly defined, the idyll is antithetical to progress.

At twenty I first recognized in myself the power of the imagination in walking. In Europe with my family for the summer, I had twice left them to wander on my own, first in Greece and a month later in Ireland. The Irish adventure directly resulted from the Greek because I had traveled in Greece with two young Irish women who subsequently entertained me in their home in County Kerry, on the shore of the Atlantic Ocean. After the train ride from Dublin to Killarney, I began on foot an uncertain thirty miles to their hamlet. Here is my 1963 diary entry of the first segment of that small journey:

Leaving Killarney after 4 P.M. I began to walk towards Kells. Shortly I was in the country first passing a superb grey cathedral with a thin pointed spire. Across the road upon which I walked were green woods with a healthy stream near the road. Moving further from the town I let my thumb fly in the breeze, but for twenty minutes nobody stopped. Finally a farmer let me sit on the fender of his tractor, and we putted along. The only casualty was suffered by my raincoat which got caught in the wheel and ripped. About six miles later he let me off, and I continued along the road. Only rarely was there a passing car or truck. More often there were passing cows. The woods lessened and turned into grazing country and farmland. Not long after I received another ride, this time from a British family. The wife said that they stopped because I looked "desperate." They took me past Killorglin and on the road to Glenbeigh. I continued my walk, now in wild country. I passed great stretches of peat bogs. In front of me were huge grey-brown mountains. The sky was grey and seeped with rain. It was towards evening and getting dark. Amidst the desolation, not really knowing where I was going, I *could* only keep going, an eye on the grand but uninviting countryside. The only sound was from the wind. A near catastrophe occurred when, while fumbling around for a map, I dropped this very diary, containing two pressed leaves from Hippocrates' plane tree picked on the Greek Island of Kos. I saved them undamaged although they fell out of the book, onto the Irish road—Greek leaves from the dry heat lying on the cold, wet Irish road.

No Wordsworthian "spot of time," none of Thoreau's reflections on summer while staring at a river frozen in water, could have amazed me more than this meeting of Greece and Ireland in my adolescent imagination. At that time I had read no Yeats and therefore had no inkling of the cultural appropriateness of this event, of my being the "guest of chance." The dull day, the walking emptiness of the world, the fallen leaf of ancient civilization, the anticipation of romance, all granted my mind the opportunity to make images out of things and motions.

III.

The episodes of my own walking that I have reported here give the genetic explanation for my preoccupation. But they do not explain why I have chosen to be thus preoccupied or why I have chosen to represent my preoccupation, to elaborate and extend it into a form of writing. Some preoccupations, after all, we choose to keep to ourselves or we choose to seek their dissolution.

The function of the guides, the Sybil and Vergil, in the *Aeneid* and *The Divine Comedy* respectively, is not only to teach and interpret to the hero the meaning of the images he sees but also to insist that imagery must not be embraced as a reality greater than the passing life. That would mean death for the hero and his failure in the present and for the future of his civilization. Psychologically the wish to embrace the image of the beloved (e.g., Patroclus for Achilles or Dido for Aeneas) is regressive, morally and socially escapist. At the same time, the hero in that wish recognizes the comic possibility of restoration or reform. The guide must facilitate the hero's conscious gaze upon the image and then—before the image totally satisfies the longings—get him walking again.

The walk is, I believe, primarily dialectical about mind and images and secondarily about action (or politics) and contemplation (or art). This is probably why so many writers and artists represent life through the setting of the walk. The preoccupation with, though not necessarily the commitment to, the image—that which fixes the gaze—belongs both to the act of walking and to art.

Not all walkers and writers about walking accept its dialectical properties and functions. Thoreau, for example, permeates the walk so completely in circularity and comedy that it becomes itself an image, it turns into art. Within this comedy appears the image of the self as a "comic" figure:" essential or unitary, impermeable to history and person, a "soul."

Far more interesting is Blake as a walker through London. The poem "London" begins with "marking" the self of the poet, but the self preoccupation dissolves in the power of the images of London's weakened citizens. Yet the images receive his sympathy in the form of his mind's freedom to observe their meaning. He "passes by," maintains his integrity yet enters the reality around him, and has the strength to represent the consciousness of his experience. This walker neither denies nor submits to experience. The walk is an engaged act of mind.

The image of the walk seems, so to speak, to undermine its status as image. It is not an image (like God, or the State, or Family) in which one can finally rest, even though many writers—particularly in the nineteenth century—may have tried. Lamb, Stevenson, Leslie Stephen, Alice Meynell, all embraced the walk as the site of the *vita contemplativa*, which they seem heartily to have preferred.

Several times a week I walk along the Highline Canal in Denver and inevitably experience in the most visceral way these dialectics of walking. The Highline Canal, built by Army Engineers from 1880 to 1883 and seventy-one miles long, was designed to carry water from the Platte River throughout the southern and eastern parts of the city. More recently the city turned fifty-eight miles of it into a recreational site. Paths—sometimes asphalt and sometimes dirt—accompany the canal for walkers, bikers, joggers, and, in places, horseback riders. Huge, dusty cottonwood trees, the massive arboreal inhabitants of this semi-arid country, also line the canal. Many parts of the canal are now enclosed in suburbia. Typically, the walker gazes into backyards just beyond the shady profusions along the banks.

As I walk, I often find myself angry, at least at the beginning of my trek. I have difficulty—apparently unknown to Thomas Mann in *A Man and His Dog*—with this suburban walking, with the paranoid sense of imprisonment in this faceless and oppressively silent society. At times I become the voyeur—not with any particular pleasure but with hostility towards the inhabitants of the dull one-story dwellings I pass by. Dylan Thomas, in "Quite Early One Morning," wrote as a voyeur imagining, as he passed through a town in Wales, the domestic tragedies and unfulfilled dreams of the people still sleeping in the houses he saw.[†] But he presented his voyeurism as wistful lyricism, as poetic beauty. I feel only rage.

Yet there are also times when the backyards appear beautiful, interesting, various. Wild roses and wild poppies grow along the fences, pumpkins and squash and corn may lie in the well-prepared gardens, flickers with black V's on their throats cross the path or hammer on cotttonwoods and telephone poles, the early-morning sun shines hard on the leaves of the trees, dogs and people pass by occasionally and the latter enjoy giving a greeting, and off to the west—as one rounds a curve in the path—appear the splendid, speckled-blue Rockies.

I know no pattern to my responses. I cannot honestly say that I begin in a rage and end in bliss, in contentment with my world and fellow creatures. Nor can I say that my obsessions or mental pleasures eventually win out over observation and social preoccupations. It may work in the reverse. I can say, however, that my experience is various and usually engages all of what I have reported, not as a blend or evolution but as a dialectic.

Or, I drive into my own thoughts unrelated to the setting, which, however, penetrate the mental theater like a spectator responding to the action on stage. No writer about the walk understands this comfortable, ever-altering restlessness better than Hazlitt, in "On Going a Journey." No essay puts forward more restlessly the Romantic walker's ambivalence toward entering the pleasurable idyll of the walk, first in nature and then on paper. Hazlitt's obvious descendants—Robert Louis Stevenson, Leslie Stephen, George Macaulay Trevelyan, and countless other and lesser walking essayists—abandon the tension originally in the Romantic artist and person in order to bathe in the intellectually less bracing waters of idyllic writing. Their minds go on holiday, and holiday is what they end up describing or, to shift the association, they describe and write for a Victorian or Edwardian men's club.

For all the spirit of restlessness in "On Going a Journey," one might imagine that, compared to his men's-club successors, Hazlitt would be inclined to erode the image of walking pleasure that the idyll obviously affords. On the contrary, Hazlitt reaches for a pleasure far more intense, not mere comfort and ease, not purely contemplative or congenial, not—finally—idyllic at all, but more erotic, more the risk of the pure present. Hazlitt's walking essay is a Romantic's argument with Romanticism. Having walked in 1798 to meet the great Romantic walkers Coleridge and Wordsworth with whom he was then identified as artists and social visionaries, he now argues against what he thinks they might say

about or do on the walk. From his point of view Coleridge and Wordsworth strove to project onto the world the inner world that they had
discovered and gloried in. Out of such projection came the idyll that
they could discover, or create, on the walk. "On Going a Journey" argues specifically against walking and talking with someone else at the
same time, for the reason that the pure unverbalized feelings of the
walker, the feelings of pleasure in a simple observation in nature, die in
a kind of awkwardness or embarrassment when they are related:

> My old friend C[oleridge], however, could do both. He could go on in the
> most delightful explanatory way over hill and dale, a summer's day, and con-
> vert a landscape into a didactic poem or a Pindaric ode. "He talked far above
> singing." If I could so clothe my ideas in sounding and flowing words, I might
> perhaps wish to have some one with me to admire the swelling theme; or I
> could be more content, were it possible for me still to hear his echoing voice
> in the woods of All-Foxden.[†]

Coleridge had the language of a poet that attracted not the mind in its
activity but in its admiration, and admiration, or wonderment, is the
preferred mental state of the idyllic walker.

From another vantage "On Going a Journey" argues about the deficien-
cies of the Romantic imagination—more extravagantly, that its powers
to create unity, to synthesize opposites, may themselves be a Romantic
construction of an idyllic mental faculty that does not really exist. Or
if it exists, it encourages not "LIBERTY, GENIUS, LOVE, VIRTUE,"
but petty nationalism and the same old entrenched world of power and
oppression.

The walk, for Hazlitt, exercises the mind in a more truly liberated
sense. The solitary walker gains entry not to the idyll at the core of
being but to more primitive thoughts and feelings. Walking, a state suspended between leaving and reconnecting with the social world that defines our character, avails us of contradiction and pain as well as pleasure; it avails intensely of the present. But this is because, strangely, it
does not strive to be anything that it is not. It has no goal of synthesis or
unity, of peace and tranquility, of pleasure without pain. Hazlitt loves
to read on his walks, but he does not go for idyllic literature but rather
for literature of passion love: *Paul and Virgina*, *The New Eloise*, *Camilla*.

He likes the Rousseauian idea of anonymity that the walk can bring, but he revises Rousseau's *amour de soi* so that it is not an idyllic but a passionate love of self that emerges. One walks not to free oneself of passion but to exercise and train the senses and the passions themselves.

Walking reminds the walker that "with change of place we change our ideas; nay, our opinions and feelings. . . . It seems we can think but of one place at a time. The canvas of the fancy has only a certain extent, and if we paint one set of objects upon it, they immediately efface every other."[†] At first it seems that Hazlitt sees the mind as limited in power. But the limitation or deflation is of Freud's kind when he says: "was man nicht erfliegen kann, muss man erhinken." In fact he only shifts the power away from those who would conceive it to lie in its capacity for visionary synthesis and utopia:

> We measure the universe by ourselves, and even comprehend the texture of our own being only piece-meal. In this way, however, we remember an infinity of things and places. The mind is like a mechanical instrument that plays a great variety of tunes, but it must play them in succession.[†]

For Hazlitt a gap separates the walk from his essay on the walk, and here he seems to differ from the purely Romantic walkers, for whom the idyllic experience of solitary walking ought, organically, to emanate in an essay equally idyllic for the reader. Hazlitt alludes to the idyllic experiences of his walks, but his essay is full of the world. He does not wish to recreate the idyll, the purity of his observations and intimations; nor does he try to speak to an "elect" of walkers, of the converted, who will merely assent in comfortable admiration. His walking essay is a piece of cultural criticism, taking walking as its occasion to respond to and explore some contemporary cultural assumptions. But Hazlitt really was a walker, and he really was an admirer of Coleridge and Wordsworth. Thus his criticism comes from one within the orbit of culture's influence: the walker as critic.

6.

The Eighteenth-Century Tour, and Beyond

Engagement and Alienation

I. Johnson, Sterne, and Wollstonecraft

Watt's way of advancing due east, for example, was to turn his bust as far as possible towards the north and at the same time to fling out his right leg as far as possible towards the south, and then to turn his bust as far as possible towards the south and at the same time to fling out his left leg as far as possible towards the north, and then again to turn his bust as far as possible towards the north and to fling out his right leg as far as possible towards the south, and then again to turn his bust as far as possible towards the south and to fling out his left leg as far as possible towards the north, and so on, over and over again, many many times, until he reached his destination, and could sit down.[†]

The world in Beckett, or Giacometti, seems empty. Only the walker defines the space, his outline, and his movement. The world provides no counter to the walker. Like a Möbius strip one distinguishes no difference between self and other. As crazy as Watt walks, the predictable geographical coordinates that his steps repeat give him comic security. How different is this from the world of eighteenth-century walkers and tourists! Beckett helps us see just how saturated older works are with color, objects (closeup and faraway), people, occasions for reflection, and drama. Consider the painting by Gainsborough, *The Morning Walk* (1785). A handsome young man and woman, sumptuously dressed, yapping dog at their side, go off in formal array through the park. Notably, the couple takes little erotic interest in one another, but the dog (usually an externalization of instinct) provides the animation its master and mistress lack. The world is full, and if the two figures do not register it, the viewer surely does.

We may think of eighteenth-century walking-tour literature as a cold genre, of interest primarily to those who have traveled the same road themselves, a genre practiced by people more committed to an abstract or at the very least now-outmoded and pale aesthetic than to real experience. But upon nearer view this prejudice vanishes. This is not to say that these overlong books cannot get tiresome, but that is owing, I suspect, to the dreary episodic nature of travel narrative and not to a lack of engagement with an engaging world. Or it may result from the difficulty one has in representing something one finds "beautiful" or "interesting." Where do we find the language, as Barthes says about the flatness of Stendhal's early tour books, for what we love? Samuel Johnson, for example, hardly anticipated a bland Tour of the Hebrides; Boswell reports: "From an erroneous apprehension of violence, Dr. Johnson had provided a pair of pistols, some gunpowder, and a quantity of bullets."[†] Johnson, indeed, is a fascinating traveler to watch because of the liveliness of his resistance to experience. It seems that he needs continuously to be persuaded:

> Dinner was mentioned.
> Johnson: "Ay, ay; amidst all these sorrowful scenes, I have no objection to dinner."[†]

This resistance leads one to appreciate even more the occasion of real connection with one's new environment. Boswell registers it wonderfully: "This is roving among the Hebrides, or nothing is."[†] And, "What an addition was it to Icolmkill to have the Rambler upon the spot!"[†]

This lovely, almost—in context—gushing, remark emphasizes how intensely human is the power of great moments on this tour. It is not solely or primarily the encounter with nature or history that scores on the walker. This is even more magically and humorously true in Sterne's

A Sentimental Journey through France and Italy. Yorick takes a few steps "in the street" in Paris, stops at a shop to ask directions. The lovely shop girl so mesmerizes the walker that he cannot summon to mind what she has told him, so—after briefly setting out on his journey—he returns to the shop to conclude by sitting next to this young woman and feeling her pulse! The moment of the encounter is always so compelling, and usually sexually compelling, that it paralyzes the walking desire. Note the gusto of:

> —What a large volume of adventures may be grasped within this little span of life by him who interests his heart in every thing, and who having eyes to see, what time and chance are perpetually holding out to him as he journeyeth on his way, misses nothing he can *fairly* lay his hands on.—[†]

> I declare, said I, clapping my hands chearily together, that was I in a desert, I would find out wherewith in it to call forth my affections—If I could not do better, I would fasten them upon some sweet myrtle, or seek some melancholy cypress to connect myself to—I would court their shade, and greet them kindly for their protection—I would cut my name upon them, and swear they were the loveliest trees throughout the desert: if their leaves wither'd, I would teach myself to mourn, and when they rejoiced, I would rejoice along with them.[†]

This is the ecstasy, not only of a picaresque hero but of a walker in love with life and kindled by life. The walker, says Sterne, opens oneself to "a parcel of nonsensical contingencies."

II. Dorothy Wordsworth

Dorothy Wordsworth—according to her brother William Wordsworth, Samuel Coleridge, and Thomas De Quincey—was the woman of the wild, wild eyes. Yet from the midnineteenth century on, readers have denied the prodigious walking, in her journals and recollections, of that wildness. She becomes the poet of the home, a kind of housekeeper of the scenes through which she passes. Even when seeking out her "identity," she does it calmly. I see, on the other hand, a walker vulnerable to erotic and visionary ecstasies. She stops to rest upon the heath: "its surface restless and glittering with the motion of the scattered piles of withered grass, and the waving of the spiders' threads." The living details of the countryside draw her into them, not like a housekeeper or even the painter of the picturesque but like a lover: no order and balance but intensity. "Grasmere looked so beautiful that my heart was almost melted away."[†] "Thus I was going on when I saw the shape of my Beloved in the road at a little distance."[†] In the earlier Alfoxden and Hamburgh journals, by contrast, she writes from a distance, in scenes. But later the scenes surround her, break down, and she sparks their elements. "As we came along Ambleside vale in the twilight it was a grave evening. There was something in the air that compelled me to serious thought—the hills were large, closed in by the sky."[†]

Do men write about their walks differently than women? one inevitably asks. Do they, more basically, walk differently? All I know about this latter is that a woman taught me how to saunter, that is, to walk at a slower, less regular pace, and my heart was almost melted away, and that it was all right, if a point in the conversation needed emphasis, to stop suddenly on the path and turn one's body and eyes and voice toward one's companion.

Would only a woman write the following?

> In a while the pitch pines close around me,
> small woods few bother to know
> with their feet.[†]

Or,

> Follow the ax cut path
> narrower than your hips
> through the labyrinth
> of trees toppled years ago
> in fire.[†]

Or,

> In wilderness, I seek the wildness in myself and in so
> doing, come on the wildness everywhere around me
> because, after all, being part of nature, I'm cut from
> the same cloth.[†]

And,

> Walking is also an ambulation of mind. The human armour
> of bones rattle, fat rolls, and inside this durable,
> fleshy prison of mine, I make a beeline towards otherness,
> lightness, or, maybe like a moth, toward flame.[†]

And,

> To find wildness, I must first offer myself up, accept
> all that comes before me:[†]

For both Marge Piercy, in her poetic sequence "Sand Roads," and Gretel
Erlich (Introduction to the Sierra Club Wilderness Calendar), the walk
envisions the body, the mind, and the world not as well-bounded en-
tities (perhaps hostile to one another) but as a gradient that signifies
well-being. This, I believe, is also true of Dorothy Wordsworth walking. When, by contrast, he walks on the dunes, A. R. Ammons ("Corson's Inlet") turns the dunes and the walk itself into metaphor:

> there are dunes of motion,
> organizations of grass, white sandy paths of remembrance
> in the overall wandering of mirroring mind:[†]

The mind on the walk grows from the anxious vision of boundaries and
constraints and thus grows content, but the representation of that contentment is abstract. The poem rests finally in philosophical statements
rising "above" the natural reality that serves it. We hear about gradients
and transitions, but the poetry itself serves to keep boundaries intact.
Walking in "Corson's Inlet" is not sexual.

The dune/ocean landscape in "Sand Roads" resists becoming metaphor and instead becomes description, drama, itself a living subject.
The poet is urged not towards the freedom of philosophical statement
but towards engagement with the landscape. Near the end she says to
herself:

> You are standing too tall for
> this landscape. Lie down.[†]

Urging herself not towards erectness and the perspectival "despotism of
the eye," entangled first in the vine of the beach pea, descending the
dunes she "lie[s] down before the ocean."

It rises over you, it stands
hissing and spreading its
cobalt hood, rattling
its pebbles.[†]

As the walker crosses the line, or blurs the line, of land and water, she creates a vision of a return to the sources of life. Air becomes earth, or rock, and water, engulfing and penetrating, deadly and life-giving. When they *lie down*, female walkers extend the walker's vision into the ecstatic realm of rebirth through the conscious welcoming of the body as a source of knowing, or relationship and touch as the way of being. Attaining this vision often occurs with the recasting of reality not into idyll but into a sometimes violent ecstasy, a sometimes (as in this passage from Dorothy Wordsworth) quiet, concentrated erotic energy:

Afterwards William lay, and I lay in the trench under the
fence—he with his eyes shut and listening to the waterfalls
and the Birds. There was no one waterfall above another—it
was the sound of waters in the air—the voice of the air.
William heard me breathing and rustling now and then but we
both lay still, and unseen by one another.[†]

III. Wordsworth, Byron, Hardy

Mary Wollstonecraft's *Letters Written during a Short Residence in Sweden, Norway, and Denmark* is one of the saddest of tour books—partly from what it communicates but mostly from what the reader knows about the occasion of its production. Sent "on business" to Scandinavia by Gilbert Imlay, her lover, who was fast becoming disaffected, and reacting with "horror" to the post-Revolutionary climate in France, she confronted this unknown land and people in a state of alienation and sorrow. The book, however, is far more vigorous and active than this situation would predict. The conditions of the societies she encounters trigger her imagination. Nature lifts her spirit; indeed, she openly acknowledges what the Romantics often forget to acknowledge—that nature is therapeutic in the face of the radical's entanglement with the burdens of social turmoil and opposition.

At this remove of almost two hundred years, what is it that we want to get from these walking writers? Surely it is not (unless we are reading as specialists) the accuracy of the description of the place and probably not even the precise spirit of the place traversed. More likely we enjoy the identification with the walker engaging the environs through which he passes. How well does the writer of the walk spark that environment into life? Does the walker participate in his or her world or is he or she alienated from it? And the most important question, how does language play in the presence of the journey?

The melancholy walker is a stereotype of eighteenth-century poetry. Reading Wordsworth's early ramble, *An Evening Walk* (1793), I expect to find an imitation of this type, but instead I am reminded that the young poet was still in his radical phase, which—in England during the Revolution—means that, amidst a solitary twilight sojourn when the natural world is supposed to be calming itself and settling down for rest, he finds light, movement, animation, and hints of sexual power, and he proves his eagerness and openness to a great and swirling variety of sensations. Miltonically, the world is all before him, and with Keats there is "wide wandering for the greediest eye," and as Wordsworth in this poem says: " 'Tis restless magic all."[†]

Walking is a feature of some radical literary writing in the 1790s. John Thelwall's three-volume *Peripatetic* is only the most famous example; walking signifies the restlessness, negatively the uprootedness and political drivenness, more positively the *mobility*, of the radical mind. Passion and sexual animation also inform this mind. Thus Wordsworth in "An Evening Walk" encounters a rooster "Sweetly ferocious," "Gazed by his sister-wives."[†] "Bright sparks his black and haggard eye-ball hurls Afar." And later on a swan:

> He swells his lifted chest, and backward flings
> His bridling neck between his tow'ring wings; . . .
> On as he floats, the silver'd waters glow,
> Proud of the varying arch and moveless form of snow.[†]

Still later, as if to show how "love of nature leads to love of man," the radical animus practiced on nature, the exercise of sexual imagination and language, reveals its (radically) logical consequence in an indignant and sympathetic portrait of an impoverished solitary mother and her helpless children.

Far more than Wordsworth on his evening walk, Byron's Childe Harold erects a meditative self at once trapped in his subjectivity ("I live and die unheard, With a most voiceless thought") and appreciative of the world through which he passes. Clarens, the setting for the passion of Rousseau's St. Preux and Julie, evokes Harold's simultaneous passion for Rousseau and nature: "Thy trees take root in Love."[†] His description of the place is very literary; he is in the land of the idyll. Wordsworth's marking of landscape and natural detail in *An Evening Walk* was praised by reviewers for its accuracy of description. Byron claims that Clarens without Rousseau still would have stimulated the sentiments of love, but it is hard to believe him. So much in these passages recurs to Rousseau and his Romantic reception and interpretation, both in the poem and in Byron's extensive note on the passage. Byron, very much here the walking poet of the principle of love ("the great principle of the universe"), does not sound like a love poet. Though the language reaches fondly into the passions of Rousseau and even of Wordsworth, the sphere of thought in which Byron/Harold is encased may find more affinity with the metaphoric walking of the grieving Tennyson of *In Memoriam*:

> I walk as ere I walk'd forlorn,
>> When all our path was fresh with dew,
>> And all the bugle breezes blew
> Reveillée to the breaking morn.[†]

or

> We pass; the path that each man trod
>> Is dim, or will be dim, with weeds.[†]

The elegy of Tennyson and the *sic transit gloria mundi* of the walker Harold leads, eventually to be sure, to Hardy's "Dead Man Walking":

> Yet is it that, though whiling
>> The time somehow
> In walking, talking, smiling,
> I live not now.[†]

It would seem that the walker Watt, with whom this chapter began, might follow from this; but I find that Beckett recalls more centrally the vigorous, engaged walkers of the late-eighteenth century. Thinking of Watt, I picture Giacometti's walkers, purposive, alive, figures of energy. The blankness of the world, the thinness of the bodies, the environment of coordinate and direction, suggest to me not a world of emptiness or deadness now but the recognition that the modern world is fundamentally confusing and contradictory; "steps" must be taken to find the path, "where to choose."

7.

"Civilization" and the Sacred

I. Hardy and Others

For many modern writers the walker becomes the person whose relationship to society has been thrown into question. Surrealists Louis Aragon (*Le Paysans de Paris*) and André Breton (*Nadja*) narrate the life of an urban walker, the intensity of whose observations and erotic, passionate visions at once disengages him from ordinary urban life and forms its critique. The "mad love" of Breton, like the passionate love of William Hazlitt for Sarah Walker in *Liber Amoris*, itself belongs to that critique of modern society as repressive of human enthusiasm and desire: the walker as Passionate Man or Woman. One of the earliest walkers in the western tradition appears in this self-imposed passionate marginality, Chryseis the prophet in the *Iliad* (Book I), whose words Agamemnon treats contemptuously and who thereafter leaves the Council of leaders to walk muttering along the shores of the Aegean.

When he encounters Socrates walking beyond the confines of the city, Phaedrus wants to engage him on the subject of love. To return to town is to enter the site of civilization containing knowledge of that which civilization fundamentally requires and yet often subdues or rejects. The walker brings the news of love back to his people.

The walker may arrive in the community as a stranger, with odd notions and plans and intense desires. He returns, as Alfred Schutz says, as "stranger" and "homecomer," at once producing a mutual attraction, a mutual wariness. How has the walker changed? remained the same? How has the community changed?

How does the walker—full of nature, desire, and the knowledge gained in his recent isolate vulnerability—engage the community? The walker belongs archetypally to the category of heroic journeyer, who in this book remains largely on the periphery of concern. Yet it is worth remarking the resonance that the most domestic of walkers has to the journeyer archetype—to Odysseus, Aeneas, and Dante—to the walker as guest, as stranger, as homecomer. Unrestricted by familiar law, custom, and taboo, forced into reexamination of self and relationship, granted an extreme immediacy before drive and desire, the walker may return to civilization with the patterns of life redrawn, the terms of life new, the urgency to remake the community deepened. This is the story of the *nostos*, or homecoming, in the *Odyssey*.

Or a walker-journeyer, by simply penetrating the confines of another civilization, may disrupt fundamentally its complacency. Having landed shipwrecked on the shores of Africa (burdened with the memory of the recently extinguished city of Troy), Aeneas and his men step out in the bright morning to walk down to the city of Carthage. Kept invisible by the gods, Aeneas can become wholly absorbed and enchanted by the beelike construction of one civilization (Carthage) and grief-stricken by the mural representation of the ugly failure of another (Troy). The self, the foreignness of the Aeneas, the hero as passionate, desiring man, only troubles the world of Carthage when the gods wipe away the mist that had kept him from the eyes of Queen Dido now standing before him.

When I observe in the ancient texts the walker-journeyer approaching the community, I sometimes become aware of a new order, the sacred. Crossing the threshold of the house, town, or city—full of nature, passion, memory, and dream—the walker enters the archetype of guest-stranger, and the host must acknowledge the embrace of the "outlandish" figure with careful ceremony and ritual. The ceremony, I believe, serves to raise to a level of the communal the fear in the walker's arrival, a fear both to the walker and to the host, that of the "other." Perhaps, as in the Agamemnon and Clytaemnestra story, the returning journeyer walks on a carpet to his murder. Perhaps, as in the Clytaemnestra and Orestes story, the returning journeyer brings murder with him. These are not gestures toward the sacred but gestures of social power and revenge. And yet there *is* the purple carpet, not only for the state welcome of the king but for that other recognition of the holiness of the return. The hope and fear are subsumed for the moment by ceremony.

In the highly nature-conscious and class-conscious world of the late-nineteenth century, Thomas Hardy begins three of his novels (*The Return of the Native, Tess of the d'Urbervilles,* and *The Mayor of Casterbridge*) with walkers on the heath approaching a community. In each case the walker's presence joins that of a communal ceremony or celebration: ritual bonfires, a May Day dance for women, a village fair. The palpable relationship of the walker to the ceremony is not (unlike the ancient texts) apparent or even particularly important, as if to suggest that in the modern world only a trace of the old meaning of the threshold remains.

These characteristic openings in Hardy predict, perhaps, that the work to follow will open up such meanings, recover their power. One learns that beneath the "natural," homely appearance of a Jack Durbeyfield resides the name d'Urberville: the "field" of the former turns out to have erased the "ville" of the latter. Beneath the natural, rough, comically repellant surface of one lies the family name of generations that means the presence of civilization. Similarly the voice of the narrator describing the desolation of the Wessex countryside through which the walker travels speaks not as do some of our current naturalist walker-writers—intent on the poetry of earth—but rather with an eye toward a civilization beneath nature or with a sense of a current "civilized" audience expecting to hear of a world strange yet belonging to one's own order. Thus the narrator of *The Return of the Native* writes at once as teller of a tale in which Egdon Heath is a character and as one who had visited it many times, a place that had elicited powerfully a philosophical, reflective impulse: he wanted to be able to say to the Heath "Civilization was its enemy" but also wanted to animate it with "watchful intentness" and observe it at dusk "slowly to awake and listen," to imagine the Roman roads beneath it, to find it "a place perfectly accordant with man's nature."[†]

When the walker encounters the community, something jostles the complacency, the obsession with continuity, in the social order: Angel walking into The Pure Drop Inn and meeting Tess, Michael Henchard walking into a "refreshment tent" at a fair and selling his wife and child.

I have been talking mostly about the solitary walker who enters the community but began with two companions—Socrates and Phaedrus—away from the city creating their own community while referring to the other one to which they belong but which currently stands some miles from them. Even though Hazlitt says he cannot bear walking and talking at the same time, many walkers like to bring civilization with them in the form of a companion or to pick up a companion on the path. Some would say, myself included, that a walking companion allows for the sharing, the crystallizing of a fuller range of thought and fantasy than does sedentary conversation, that, in other words, one can gratify some of the walking desire—an opening up of the self to oneself—more fully by "civilizing" with another. But just as a turn in the road may alter my view and thereby shift or remold my thinking, so does the walking conversation produce something far different from a train of associations.

A walker typically likes to cultivate anonymity on a journey. This pleasure comes from accepting for the moment at least that society is a burden to be from time to time cast off so that one can recover the "sole self" and the energy and the peace that comes with that recovery. The correlate social pleasure derives from conversing-in-anonymity, sometimes with one from a different class, so that we discover we are "all of one human society." No writer taps this impulse more effectively than Williams Wordsworth with his repeated encounters with poor, rural figures. Beset with anxiety and overwhelmed with fantasy about his durability in his poethood, the poet meets on the hills the strange, ancient Leechgatherer who—as they talk—organizes and subdues the poet's turbulence into an image of wandering firmness. The effect of the encounter, as the poet tells it, is finally spiritual, mystical, admonitory, more than social. Half the time the old man's words pass by, or through, the poet "like a stream scarce heard." Interestingly, an early draft of this poem shows that Wordsworth was far more taken with the physical and social particulars of the Leechgatherer than in the final version, as if to say that "civilization" is the absorption of social into spiritual experience, that the "human society" meets on this level and not on this level of social difference. At least this is the walker's privilege.

II. Basho: The Narrow Road to the Deep North

In this little book of travel is included everything under the sky—not only that which is hoary and dry but also that which is young and colourful, not only that which is strong and imposing but also that which is feeble and ephemeral. As we turn every corner of the Narrow Road to the Deep North, we sometimes stand up unawares to applaud and we sometimes fall flat to resist the agonizing pains we feel in the depths of our hearts. There are also times when we feel like taking to the road ourselves, seizing the raincoat lying near by, or times when we feel like sitting down till our legs take root, enjoying the scene we picture before our eyes. Such is the beauty of this little book that it can be compared to the pearls which are said to be made by the weeping mermaids in the far-off sea. What a travel it is indeed that is recorded in this book, and what a man he is who experienced it. The only thing to be regretted is that the author of this book great man as he is, has in recent years grown old and infirm with hoary frost upon his eyebrows.[†]

To the Western reader to analyze or demystify such a statement of the beautiful seems trivial and misguided. The efforts of some, like Basho, to sift out the elemental curves of life, to announce the existence of such curves that follow the elemental road, to define the life as blessed with solitude, yet bestowing and receiving hospitality, simply marks the beauty of an ordered life that gives and receives in dignity. The book is, makes, the beautiful life. As such it is like a pearl, secret and dear. There are those books we know and guard as jewels.

For all the detail of place and character in Basho's *The Narrow Road to the Deep North*, the two-and-a-half-year and three-thousand-mile walk recounted in prose and haiku is about the divine, the traditional, and the poetic all encountered, imagined, and produced on the walk. Basho does not deny the psychological experience of walking or the need for wandering, but he prefers:

> As firmly cemented clam-shells
> Fall apart in autumn,
> So I must take to the road again,
> Farewell, my friends.[†]

And,

> It looks as if
> Iris flowers had bloomed
> On my feet—
> Sandals laced in blue.[†]

Once some concubines stopped him on the road: "We are forlorn travellers, complete strangers on this road. Will you be kind enough at least to let us follow you?" Their "life was such that they had to drift along even as the white froth of waters that beat on the shore. . . . " To journey on the road to the Deep North is more purposeful, to enter in this life a place of mystery, of almost "pure" civilization, a place marked by poets and the memories and artifacts of ancient warriors and leaders. It seems in this sense to have affinities with our poets' underworld journeys. Basho reveals that inherently literary principle of his walk by writing poems to commemorate his visit and by excusing himself when circumstances make him unable to write. This gesture of contact between poet and place seems to be the common fact of these poems, which can range from description to psychological expression and philosophical observation:

> Rid of my hair,
> I came to Mount Kurokami,
> On the day we put on
> Clean summer clothes.[†]

Or,

> Amid mountains of high summer,
> I bowed respectfully before
> The tall clogs of a statue,
> Asking a blessing on my journey.[†]

Or,

> A thicket of summer grass
> Is all that remains
> Of the dreams and ambitions
> Of ancient warriors.[†]

Or,

I am awe-struck
To hear a cricket singing
Underneath the dark cavity
of an old helmet.[†]

Or,

No matter where I fall
On the road,
Fall will I to be buried
Among flowering bush-clovers.[†]

In one of Hermann Hesse's few unpretentious books, *Wandering* (1920), the piety of Basho becomes "trust," the contentment of the Romantic walker with the natural world, a contentment of the solitary who lives in wishes and maternal longings and memory. As Basho quotes his ancestors, so Hesse recalls the poet Eichendorff:

Soon, oh how soon the still time will come,
When I too will rest, and over me
Will rustle the lovely loneliness of trees,
And, even here, no one will know me.

I perceive for the first time [Hesse adds] that even in this beloved passage the sadness is merely the shadow of a cloud. This sadness is nothing but the gentle music of passing things, and without it, whatever is beautiful does not touch us. It is without pain. I take it with me on my journey, and I feel contented as I step briskly farther up the mountain path, the lake far below me, past a mill brook with chestnut trees and a sleeping mill wheel, into the quiet blue day.[†]

Such pearls of consolation rimmed with mild sadness, reducing the world and the mind to the beauty of the distant lake, the mountain path, and the quiet blue day appeal to me, beckon me, out of the simple ease of their vision and execution. I long to repeat it in my own writing from time to time, to become this walker-writer. The notion of "idyll" seems inappropriately applied to Basho. Perhaps it is wrong of me to link Hesse and Basho in one brief essay. The former I find a stepping stone to the latter. One in good conscience and in the long run cannot wish for Hesse's world; we know too well what human monsters that intense

acceptance of aesthetic innocence can produce. Basho's piety, his stepping into eternity on the walk—if that is what it is—does not require
the reduction in intensity of the outer and inner worlds through which
he passes. His devotion to the road does not, however, always please
me: he rebuffs the concubines, telling them to find salvation by themselves; he has too much to do for himself on his own journey.

8.

The Walk as Comedy

At length, as we plodded along the dusty roads, our thoughts became as dusty as they; all thought indeed stopped, thinking broke down, or proceeded only passively in a sort of rhythmical cadence of the confused material of thought, and we found ourselves mechanically repeating some familiar measure which timed with our tread.[†]

Reducing thought to its confused material coincides with a larger, more pervasive theme in Thoreau and Emerson, that of forgetting the past in order to experience fully the present. It is a point made briefly by Hazlitt (and to my knowledge not at all by other English walkers) but for the different purpose of establishing a fact about the mind's limitation (" . . . we forget [the scenes] that we have just left. It seems that we can think but on one place at a time"). The walk satisfies us by conforming to the natural limitation of the mind. For the nineteenth-century Americans, by contrast, forgetting is the mental condition that liberates us into the only experience of life worth living, the fresh encounter with the new and the wild. Every step of the walk unburdens us of what we have just seen and thought while it simultaneously thrusts us into the previously unknown. This novelty into which he travels assures the walker of singing in a major key. The prophetic voice of Emerson ("Men walk as prophecies of the next age")[†] sounds the characteristic note in "Circles":

> In nature every moment is new; the past is always swallowed and forgotten; the coming only is sacred. Nothing is secure but life, transition, the energizing spirit. No love can be bound by oath or covenant to secure it against a higher love. No truth so sublime but it may be trivial to-morrow in the light of new thoughts. People wish to be settled; only as far as they are unsettled is there any hope for them.[†]

And once again:

> The one thing which we seek with insatiable desire is to forget outselves, to be surprised out of our propriety, to lose our sempiternal memory and to do something without knowing how or why; in short to draw a new circle. Nothing great was ever achieved without enthusiasm. The way of life is wonderful; it is by abandonment.[†]

Thoreau pursues the same idea in "Walking," when he accounts for his apparent "instinct" for stepping westward by associating the west with the new frontier, both of the nation and of the mind. The future, which for Emerson is the only time zone charged with significance and erotic power, is in the west. Even if the walk lasts for only a few hours and a few miles, it can, if it is westward, confirm this universal tendency of the unfolding American narrative. To participate in this tendency demands a forgetting:

> We go eastward to realize history and study the works of art and literature, retracing the steps of the race; we go westward as into the future, with a spirit of enterprise and adventure. The Atlantic is a Lethean stream, in our passage over which we have had an opportunity to forget the Old World and its institutions.[†]

Forgetting produces a spontaneity, a sense of the childlike, a genuineness of spirit and a capacity for "sympathy with intelligence." Thoreau would rather have us ignorant and available to life (indeed availability to life demands some ignorance) than rooted and sodden with knowledge. It is extraordinary that neither writer seems to have the faintest notion of (or is it interest or belief in?) repression. There is no residue, no baggage of the past, no malignancy or even coloring from experience when one is truly living, as if a walker hiking over soft ground would leave no footprints behind him. Walking, the activity that literally and symbolically liberated us into the future, becomes our most effective Lethe, eradicating all traces of a previous life with each step we take. All "repressed" energy and knowledge seems to flow into the activity of walking itself, the receptivity of the life we pass by and through, and the stimulation of an "inner walk" of the mind, the mind free and full in the future tense.

Both Emerson and Thoreau conceive of the circle as the image in which this wholeness of mind and body bursts from the willed forgetting. Emerson's inspired essay, "Circles," elaborates a philosophy of becoming (step by step, beginning after beginning), which encounters being at every step:

> The eye is the first circle; the horizon which it forms is the second; and throughout nature this primary figure is repeated without end. It is the highest emblem in the cipher of the world. St. Augustine described the nature of God as a circle whose center was everywhere and its circumference nowhere. We are all our lifetime reading the copious sense of this first of forms. One moral we have already deduced in considering the circular or compensatory character of every human action. Another analogy we shall now trace, that every action admits of being outdone. Our life is an apprenticeship to the truth that around every circle another can be drawn; that there is no end in nature, but every end is a beginning; that there is always another dawn risen on mid-noon, and under every deep a lower deep opens.[†]

We are walking through circles and on their path at the same time, encountering wholeness, creating it, experiencing it. Life fully lived is the mandala, the uroboric dream. Thoreau's profound commitment to the walk as the emblem of human life at its most real and gratifying coincides with Emerson on circles. Not only does the walk stimulate a continual sense of renewal, but the terrain of the walk, to the walker, becomes the experience of the circle ("You may go round the world / By the Old Marlborough Road").[†] Resting in the morning on the top of a hill (in "A Walk to Wachusett"), he saw with an Emersonian eye the map of the land, out from and below him, through which he would soon be traveling: "On every side, the eye ranged over successive circles of towns, rising one above another, like the terraces of a vineyard, till they were lost in the horizon."[†]

The walk begins quickly to suggest that life has become symbolic, poetic. "Literature," says Emerson, "is a point outside of our hodiernal circle through which a new one may be described."[†] On the way to becoming literature, the walk passes through mind. Thoreau would collapse any hard distinctions between a physical walk, an "inner walk," and the walk of a truly wild (new) piece of writing. They are all simply different stages of human life realizing itself. In the beautiful essay, "A Winter Walk," Thoreau creates a sentence to describe the beginning of his walk (the essay itself had opened with a paragraph on the "end" of night and the "beginning" of day), such that the first steps seem to generate a perception of life "circling" around and within him:

> Opening the gate, we tread briskly along the lone country road, crunching the dry and crisped snow under our feet, or aroused by the sharp, clear creak of the wood-sled, just starting for the distant market, from the early farmer's door, where it has lain the summer long, dreaming amid the chips and stubble; while far through the drifts and powdered windows we see the farmer's early candle, like a paled star, emitting a lonely beam, as if some severe virtue were at its matins there.[†]

In that inner walk (which becomes the walking essay) the sense of circularity matures. "A Winter Walk" celebrates one of the genuine pleasures of walking, an exercise of the circular imagination that envisions summer while it walks through winter, creating a perfectly integrated circuit between body and mind. The essay constantly renews this circuit before our eyes: "Meanwhile we step hastily along through the powdery snow, warmed by an inward heat, enjoying an Indian summer still, in the increased glow of thought and feeling."[†] The climax is reached when Thoreau skates over a frozen "meandering" stream and both sees and imagines summer under the wintry surface of ice:

> No domain of nature is quite closed to man at all times, and now we draw near to the empire of the fishes. Our feet glide swiftly over unfathomed depths, where in summer our line tempted the pout and perch, and where the stately pickerel lurked in the long corridors formed by the bulrushes. The

deep, impenetrable marsh, where the heron waded and bittern squatted, is made pervious to our swift shoes, as if a thousand railroads had been made into it. With one impulse we are carried to the cabin of the muskrat, that earliest settler, and see him dart away under the transparent ice, like a furred fish, to his hole in the bank; and we glide rapidly over meadows where lately 'the mower whet his scythe,' through beds of frozen cranberries mixed with meadow-grass.[†]

It should be clear that, by showing him life beneath the surface of winter—hints of the opposite season—nature encourages Thoreau on his inner walk. As much as the walk turns into a verbal excursion, equally does it tend to exert in the opposite direction, that language be smoothed to the contours of nature: the distinctly human needs to be subdued. When someone is chopping down trees in the woods, "all elements strive to naturalize the sound." As the snow begins to fall heavily again, he remarks: "With so little efforts does Nature reassert her rule and blot out the traces of man." And as if to affirm that the reader of the essay is by definition also a walker who in turn reads nature, Thoreau begins a paragraph: "But now, while we have loitered. . . ."[†]

Roland Barthes has said: "It is because I forget that I read." An essay that attempts to become a walk encourages the principle of forgetting in reading. On a walk one is continually encountering the new and, by the "despotism of the eye," the tyranny of bodily pleasure, willingly forgetting the old. Every forgetting is an assertion of freedom from which the mind goes on another journey. Every forgetting is, in addition, a self-forgetting, an assertion of renewed innocence and pleasure. As we forget, and forget ourselves, we become aware of the gradual fact of hoarding of encounters, impressions, and discoveries. We begin to experience our world as a growing plenitude; the circular imagination is also an autumnal one.

A work that fully realizes the literary walker's forgettings and cumulations is that subtlest of walking poems, Keats's "To Autumn." The final stanza shows us that our horizontal (walking, forgetting) motions have their vertical (inner, imaginative, cumulative) components or compensations. The questions insistently put forth at the beginning of the last stanza ("Where are the songs of Spring? Ay, where are they?"), questions which demand connections and rememberings, are then dismissed

("Think not of them, thou has thy music too,—"). The speaker here is rewarded for his forgetting with a gathering of music, a pluralizing of sounds around an instant on a walk.[†]

The autumnal walk of Keats celebrates the truth of change, our fear of change, and the mind's power to accept change through ordering it. A. R. Ammons' *Corson's Inlet* is a modern autumnal walking poem that hints that the resistances to the mind's and heart's ease are to be found in the terrors of intrusion:

> no arranged terror: no forcing of image, plan,
> or thought:
> no propaganda, no humbling of reality to precept:
>
> terror pervades but is not arranged.[†]

In Wallace Stevens's language, the sounds of autumn here become "keener sounds," and for Keats, Stevens, and Ammons the "arranged terror" begins to dissolve the walk and be replaced by a poetic gathering of sounds. Ammons's poem begins:

> I went for a walk over the dunes again this morning
> to the sea,
> then turned right along
> the surf
> rounded a naked headland
> and returned
> along the inlet shore.[†]

What Stevens calls the "ever-hooded, tragic-gestured sea," "the water never formed to mind or voice" ("The Idea of Order at Key West"),[†] is what Ammons turns from. Like the singer in Stevens, this speaker repeats that walk along the ocean and then turns inland, away from the sea, which then loses its force. Inland, at merely one remove from the sea, is one possibility of a precise imagery, an occasion for the keener observations and sounds of the naturalist poet encountering the realer terror of animal life preying on itself. This is an emblem of the evolutionary process in which he participates and in which he could easily sink to a vision of his own participation in evolution not as order but as an entropic chaos of mindless instinct for survival. The question forming precariously, dangerously, as he walks along the sea concerns the

ultimate power of imagination—Thoreau's language of the inner walk—
to defeat the tyranny of the animal and the tyranny of the rational
(that is, the "perpendiculars, / straight lines, blocks, boxes, binds / of
thought" . . .).[†]

It is here where Ammons draws heavily on the naïve but compelling
visions of his American predecessors, Emerson and Thoreau. For Ammons's walk describes the circle of liberation, the circle that brings novelty and the sense of wholeness all at once. Yet as the magic circle approaches, it shades, eddies into wholeness by an infinite gathering of
moments, of walks. He states that his freedom lies in the fact that

> Scope eludes my grasp, that there is no finality of vision,
> that I have perceived nothing completely,
> that tomorrow a new walk is a new walk.[†]

The final line speaks not only to the impossibility of total knowledge
but to the possibility of forgetting, of extending one's naïveté "again," as
he says at the beginning of the poem, into his walk. The sense of danger
is greater in Ammons than in Keats or in the earlier Americans. He says,
in a synthesis of the tradition: "risk is full."[†]

9.

Walking and Solitude

I. Rousseau

With Kafka, Giacometti, and other moderns eventually to appear in these notes we learn about ourselves as urban walkers, walkers as citizens, walkers as psyches vulnerable to nightmare and fear but open to the variety and tenacity of the human community. Rousseau, however, has taught us that in walking we may feel like lords and ladies of the earth. We approach a condition of being, the mind fills the landscape or may surpass it:

> Never did I think so much, exist so vividly, and experience so much, never have I been so much myself—if I may use that expression—as in the journeys I have taken alone and on foot. There is something about walking which stimulates and enlivens my thoughts. When I stay in one place I can hardly think at all; my body has to be on the move to set my mind going. The sight of the countryside, the succession of pleasant views, the open air, a sound appetite, and the good health I gain by walking, the easy atmosphere of an inn, the absence of everything that makes me feel my dependence, of everything that recalls me to my situation—all these serve to free my spirit, to lend a greater boldness to my thinking, to throw me, so to speak, into the vastness of things, so that I can combine them, select them, and make them mine as I will, without fear or restraint. I dispose of all Nature as its master.

My heart, as it strays from one object to another, unites and identifies itself with those which soothe it, wraps itself in pleasant imaginings, and grows drunk on feelings of delight. If, in order to hold them, I amuse myself by describing them to myself, what vigorous brush-strokes, what freshness of colour, what energy of expression I bring to them! All this, I am told, people have found in my works, although they have been written in my declining years. Oh, if only they had seen those of my early youth, those I sketched during my travels, those I composed but never wrote down! Why do I not write them, you will ask. But why should I? I reply. Why rob myself of the present charm of their enjoyment, to tell others that I enjoyed them once? What did readers matter to me, or a public, or the whole world, while I was soaring in the skies? Besides, did I carry paper with me, or pens? If I had thought of all that, nothing would have come to me. I did not foresee that I should have ideas. They arrive when they please, not when it suits me. Either they do not come at all, or they come in a swarm, overwhelming me with their strength and their numbers. Ten volumes a day would not have been enough. How could I have found time to write them? When I arrived, my only thought was for a good dinner. When I set out, I thought only of a good walk. I felt that a fresh paradise was waiting for me at the inn door. I thought only of going out to find it.[†]
Confessions, Book IV

Who would ever wish to paint what he saw on the walk, or write about it? The walk itself is its own expression. No words are needed. No objects, finally, exist since they are absorbed into the subject. In the walk there is no need to signify anything. Passion no longer signifies an object since passion for once is pure satisfaction. Only love of nature, love of the mind, and love of the self exist. Rousseau's famous distinction between *amour propre* and *amour de soi* comes clear on the walk. *Amour propre* is passion that insinuates itself in the world of people and objects. Ambition, sexual desire, possession, jealousy, anger, self-pity, and devaluation all contribute, says Rousseau, to our belittlement and to the belittlement of our world. *Amour de soi* is a love of self that can only be called good. With *Amour de soi* we discover the healthy narcissistic love that gives us the feeling of well-being and trust. At the core of our being, he proposes, lies a special feeling, the "sentiment of existence." On the walk in nature we reduce ourselves to this sentiment, a reduction which is also an expansion.

In *Emile*, Rousseau's awesome excursus on an ideal education, the ideal young man meets the ideal young lady, Sophie, on a walk. Having grown up past adolescence into a serene maturity, the younger walker has within himself the leisure and discernment to receive and dispose of the pleasures of nature first like a philosopher and then like the benign landlord he will become. Nature is his "museum." In this state of mind he arrives at a small, neat house in the wood. Convinced that he is received with gracious Homeric hospitality, he enters the house of Sophie and her parents. "To travel on foot," Rousseau says, "is to travel like Thales, Plato, and Pythagoras."[†] The walk of the young philosopher with his caution-conscious tutor leads him into an idyll of love and eventually marriage.

The education of Emile is, like that in Plato's *Republic*, ideal, and so is his walk and its consequences. Behind this walk and in the walking of the *Confessions* and *Reveries of the Solitary Walker* lies the persecutory fear that dogs Rousseau's step. In the *Reveries* he makes it clear that the pleasure of the walk increases with his certainty of persecution and the severity of measures he has taken to separate himself from society. The pleasure of the walk covers Rousseau's inner emptiness. One incident in the *Reveries* betrays his ambivalence about walking. Having taken a long excursion into the mountains and having walked deeper and deeper into wilds, he "sat down on a cushion of *Lycopodium* and mosses and began to dream more at ease thinking that I was in a refuge unknown to the whole universe where persecutors would not unearth me. A flash of pride soon inserted itself into this reverie. I compared myself to those great travelers who discover an uninhabited island, and I said to myself with self-satisfaction: 'Without a doubt, I am the first mortal to have penetrated thus far.' I saw myself almost as another Columbus." This grandiose fantasy, so ready at hand to any walker in the wilds, swiftly vanishes: "While I preened myself with this idea, I heard, not far from me, a certain clanking I thought I recognized; I listened—the same noise was repeated and increased. Surprised and curious, I got up, burst through a thicket of brush on the side from which the noise was coming, and, in a little valley twenty feet from the very place where I believed myself to have been the first to arrive, I saw a stocking mill." What must have been somewhat unusual in the 1760s is now terribly common for the walker seeking the "untrodden way" in the midst of civilization. But Rousseau's response is at least as interesting as the incident itself is funny and pathetic:

> I cannot express the confused and contradictory emotions which this discovery stirred up in me. My first reaction was one of joy at finding myself among humans where I had thought I was quite alone. But this reaction, which came like a flash of lightning, quickly gave way to a more lasting feeling of distress at not being able, even in the depths of the Alps, to escape from the cruel hands of men intent on persecuting me.[†]

For all of Rousseau's cultivation of persecution (some of which persecution was surely warranted), he longs for the company from which his walk is designed to protect him. On the walk he wants to approximate that state of being and unity, the sentiment of existence, that he finds on Saint Peter's Island, a condition of complete spiritual self-sufficiency. (A curious comparison of Rousseau in these *Reveries* and Hazlitt in "On Going a Journey" is that both writers praise the self-sufficiency of walking solitude but write contentiously about it.) Yet who would expect this lover of solitary walking to welcome the sound of human voices? Only after he thinks about it does he revert to the position of suffocation and paranoia. This, I think, shows that no matter how much he loved walking, Rousseau wrote about it as a reactive phenomenon. Thus he can wish for the walk to be a "happy prison." He prefers his Saint Peter's Island walks above all others because the Swiss government has imprisoned him in a freedom of movement on the island.

Rousseau's walks are expressions of power. He is controlled by the Swiss government, and he in turn controls the "colony" of rabbits on the island. He also "controls" the plant life here. The pleasure of botanizing for Rousseau is the pleasure of analyzing. All plants are subject to his or Linneaus's categories, which he subdues by knowing them. He walks through his kingdom, paying his respects to his subjects.

II. The Houseless Walker

A house or cave or cloak of imagination, a distance from objects, allows most walkers to dwell in an inner space for their wandering. This protection or "aura" is the Romantic element of the walk, a given on the walks of Rousseau and Wordsworth. Dickens claims that he is "house-less" in his "Night Walks" through London (see below), but as startled as he may be by the apparitions of the late-night and early-morning hours, he retains the inner warmth of the sheltered pedestrian spectator. But when the forty-eight-year-old poet John Clare—wandering in mind and poverty-stricken—escapes the madhouse to wander some miles to his home, imagining around the bend his love of years past, he describes a figure much more vulnerable in body and mind than other walkers who have told their stories. The ground, the weather, the distances, the path and directions, his stomach, and his mind conspire to make the six-day "journey out of Essex" a singular discomfort, a gnawing intrusion. Compared to other walkers who fill their minds with sights and associations, nobody is as lonely as John Clare.

He begins: "I walked down the lane gently. . . . " Perhaps this is more a wish for his walk than the reality—the soft, mollified relationship between ground and foot:

> I walked down the lane gently and was soon in Enfield Town and bye and bye on the great York Road where it was all plain sailing and steering ahead meeting no enemy and fearing none I reached Stevenage where being Night I got over a gate crossed over the corner of a green paddock where seeing a pond or hollow in the corner I forced to stay off a respectable distance to keep from falling into it for my legs were nearly knocked up and began to stagger.[†]

Unable to get through a sentence of gentle walking without his legs beginning to give way, Clare opens his verbal ramble that is more a stumble of misfortune and misdirection. Most walkers possess *something*: health, energy, acuteness of mind, a degree of sensuous delicacy and piquancy, fullness of imagination, the freedom—when walking alone—to create for themselves a community of images and associations. For Clare the walk merely insults the Romantic energies of mind and body. With each step he sheds more of the walker's comfort and approaches and fastens onto that houseless state of the outcast. Most walkers cultivate their wishes, but for Clare

> the road on the left hand was quite over shaded by some trees and quite dry so I sat down half an hour and made a good many wishes for breakfast but wishes was no hearty meal so I got up as hungry as I sat down—[†]

As he wishes for food, so he wishes for directions, but the basic coordinates of landscape seem to elude him:

> I then suddenly forgot which was North or South and though I narrowly examined both ways I could see no tree or bush or stone heap that I could recollect [*sic*] I had passed so I went on mile after mile almost convinced I was going the same way I came and these thoug[h]ts were so strong upon me that doubt and hopelessness made me turn so feeble that I was scarcely able to walk yet I could not sit down or give up but shuffled along. . . . [†]

> I then got up and pushed onward seeing little to notice for the road very often looked as stupid as myself.[†]

During a bitter and wet three weeks in November and December, 1974, the moviemaker Werner Herzog chose to walk alone from Munich to Paris. He walked along highways and through towns, ate at truck stops and roadside restaurants, slept in inns but also broke into a couple of empty summer cottages. He tramped over mountains and through soggy valley trails.

The reason for his journey is astounding. Word came to him that Lotte Eisner, the German film critic, was dying in Paris. He believed that to walk to her hospital bed would keep her alive. For this he needed to invest himself with enormous power:

> One solitary overriding thought: get away from here. People frighten me. Our Eisner must not die, she will not die, I won't permit it. She is not dying now because she is not dying. Not now, no, she is not allowed. My steps are firm. And now the earth trembles. When I move, a buffalo moves. When I rest, a mountain reposes. She wouldn't dare! She mustn't. She won't. When I'm in Paris she will be alive. She must not die. Later, perhaps, when we allow it.[†]

Herzog is an urban walker but not in the tradition of either a Baudelaire or a Reznikoff. The environment through which he walks does not enter him with metaphysical or ideological hostility. Although the objects of the modern industrial world with its profligate waste appear on the journey, they are not loaded with either the hostility of the social critic or the aura of love and protection of the urban Romantic. They seem more like reminders of home, steadying markers of familiarity also occasioning the pleasure of detached observation:

The cigarette packages on the roadside fascinate me greatly, even more when left uncrushed, then blown up slightly to take on a corpse-like quality, the edges no longer so sharp and the cellophane dimmed from inside from the dampness forming water droplets in the cold.[†]

I read this book looking for such signs of comfort because the trip—as Herzog repeatedly notes—is so lonely. The loneliness seems exacerbated by the harshness of the elements—rain, sleet, snow, cold wind—and the pains in his foot and leg: "Why is walking so full of woe?"[†] Nothing is sensational, nothing encountered renders a permanent inner change. The walker's mind forever expands to fit in strange sights; he has a very pliable receptivity. Is this part of the loneliness, the wayward and boundless expansion of the organs of perception? This sensitive openness to the objects before him probably makes him feel as though he is forever in someone else's home, someone else's neighborhood comfort. Yet part of living in modern technology is knowing that distance does not have to be isolating. This knowledge cuts through my sympathy with the walker's solitude and isolation, when Herzog stops somewhere along the road simply to make a call home to his wife, or when he notes in a town that one of his movies is showing there. But beyond all this is the love animating his walk, Lotte Eisner. The book has a comic plot, ending in Madame Eisner's hospital room:

I was embarrassed and placed my smarting legs up on a second armchair, which she pushed over to me. In the embarrassment, a thought passed through my head, and since the situation was strange anyway, I told it to her. Together, I said, we shall boil fire and stop fish. Then she looked at me and smiled very delicately, and since she knew that I was alone on foot and therefore unprotected, she understood me. For one splendid fleeting moment something mellow flowed through my deadly tired body. I said to her, open the window, from these last days onward I can fly.[†]

10.

Night Walks

Anne Finch, Countess of Winchilsea, wrote "A Nocturnal Reverie" in which she wants night to bring "the free soul to a composedness charmed, / Finding the elements of rage disarmed." Composedness—from one point of view an integration of self and from another a retreat—occasions composition, perhaps a poetry that longs for a divine communion ("silent musings urge the mind to seek / Something, too high for syllables to speak"),[†] or at least the sublunary poetry of the nightwalker. These eighteenth-century British poets (e.g., Finch, Thomas Parnell, Mark Akenside, Edward Young, William Collins, Joseph Warton) worship night and melancholy, the goddess of night, and Philomela. They seek a beauty that displaces grief and loneliness and that values "contemplation" as a mortal substitute for direct commerce with the music of the spheres. Contemplation comes from Milton's penseroso figure:

> . . . divinest Melancholy,
> Whose Saintly visage is too bright
> To hit the Sense of human sight;
> And therefore to our weaker view,
> O'erlaid with black, staid Wisdom's hue.[†]

Poetry comes from the blackness, the dark pause between the shining moon of classical poetic inspiration and the morning sun that forces one out of poetry and into cares, both sun and moon at this moment in history curtailing rather than encouraging the poet's activity. Such nighttime poetry should, we might think, bring us to the poet's inner life, to dreams and those dimensions of the self that seem to contradict one's self-image, but this poetry rarely travels so far.

The city night walk as satire includes Johnson's "London" and its origins in John Gay's *Trivia: or, The Art of Walking the Streets of London* (1716), Book II, "Of Walking the Streets by Night," which in turn recalls Juvenal's *Satire III*. In these poems the noxious features of the city are so literally real that a walk consists of dodging the impediments to uninterrupted motion. "Respice nunc alia ac diversa pericula noctis—."[†] And now regard the different and diverse dangers of the night. One must, according to Juvenal, avoid slo-basins emptied from an open window, beams falling from buildings consumed by fire, and the threats of drunken madmen. Gay's *Trivia* establishes the entire elaboration of his theme around the *pericula noctis*: "Let constant vigilance thy footsteps guide, / And wary circumspection guard thy side." Danger is not only physical but moral as well: "Oh! may thy virtue guard thee through the roads / Of Drury's mazy courts, and dark abodes, / The harlots' guileful paths. . . ."[†] *Satire III*, *Trivia*, and "London" all describe the destructive conflagration of the city, Juvenal and Gay alluding to the conflagration of Troy. For the satirists, of course, no hero receives a visionary education (e.g. Aeneas) in the process. The city does not die to make room for a greater one embraced by destiny. Yet Gay draws the moral from his poem and sketches the redemption which his poem can afford:

> Consider, reader, what fatigues I've known,
> The toils, the perils of the wintry town;
> What riots seen, what bustling crouds I bor'd,
> How oft I cross'd where carts and coaches roar'd;
> Yet shall I bless my labours, if mankind
> Their future safety from my dangers find.
> Thus the bold traveller . . .
> Sets forth his journals to the public view,
> To caution, by his woes, the wand'ring crew.[†]

Gay prescribes caution for the wandering crew that enters the city: maintain your distance, avoid the dangers of the night, and you will protect yourself. We find a kind of protective imagination operating both here and in the melancholy country nightwalker. The problem for the walker involves a sympathetic engagement with the world in his path—not any vague or imagined "otherness" but the houseless human community of the urban night. The city nightwalk dramatizes the loss of distance between observer and observed, between the interpreter and the object of the interpretation, between the concerns of the self in terms that the self approves and the concerns of others who, in the consciousness of the observer, suffer from various economic and spiritual distortions at the hands of a more privileged class.

In his essay, "A City Night Piece," Oliver Goldsmith shows a late eighteenth-century mind suddenly confronting the gap between his classical dream of reality and that which asserts itself before his eyes and beckons him forward. It opens:

> The clock has just struck two, the expiring taper rises and sinks in the socket, the watchman forgets the hour in slumber, the laborious and the happy are at rest, and nothing wakes but meditation, guilt, revelry, and despair. The drunkard once more fills the destroying bowl, the robber walks his midnight round, and the suicide lifts his guilty arm against his own sacred person.
>
> Let me no longer waste the night over the page of antiquity, or the sallies of contemporary genius, but pursue the solitary walk, where vanity, ever changing, but a few hours past walked before me, where she kept up the pageant, and now, like a froward child, seems hushed with her own importunities.[†]

Like the visionary dream in the underworld, the city night walk reveals the city's own underworld. "Vanity" no longer mediates between the observer and the unpleasant truths of the city. Goldsmith rejects, at this unlikely hour, the mediation of language—ancient or modern—for the immediacy of his own walk. But before he sees what the streets hold, he meditates in nearly formulaic language on the shortness of life and civilization:

> What cities, as great as this, have once triumph'd in existence, had their victories as great, joy as just, and as unbounded, and with short-sighted presumption, promised themselves immortality. Posterity can hardly trace the situation of some. The sorrowful traveller wanders over the awful ruins of others, and as he beholds, he learns wisdom, and feels the transience of every sublunary possession.[†]

One feels in this Goldsmith the friend of Dr. Johnson for whom "sleep is equally a leveller with Death; that the time is never at a great distance, when the balm of rest shall be effused alike upon every head, when the diversities of life shall stop their operation, and the high and the low shall lie down together."[†]

But Goldsmith is not fated to rest in the luxury of these melancholic contemplations, for he begins to see and is horrified by what he sees: "strangers, wanderers, and orphans, whose circumstances are too humble to expect redress, and whose distresses are too great even for pity. . . . Some are without the covering even of rags, and others emaciated with disease. . . . "[†] The rest of the essay is strikingly more troubled than the first half, Goldsmith experiencing a rush of confused feelings connected to the poverty of the night creatures and to his sense of impotence with respect to their misery:

> Why why was I born a man, and yet see the sufferings of wretches I cannot relieve! Poor houseless creatures! the world will give you reproaches, but will not give you relief. The slightest misfortunes of the great, the most imaginary uneasinesses of the rich, are aggravated with all the power of eloquence, and held up to engage our attention and sympathetic sorrow. The poor weep un- heeded, persecuted by every subordinate species of tyranny, and every law, which gives others security, becomes an enemy to them.
>
> Why was this heart of mine formed with so much sensibility! or why was not my fortune adapted to its impulse! Tenderness, without a capacity of re- lieving, only makes the man who feels it more wretched than the object which sues for assistance.[†]

"A City Night-Piece" is truly an "essay," an experiment or trial in feelings that lead the speaker astray on his walk. He confronts the trap of his own social position in which his feelings lead out toward another's mis- ery but cannot touch it, a condition that leaves him more isolated than ever. Goldsmith seems caught between two opposing but effectual ways of responding to poverty: the satirical and the visionary. The former respects objects as other, while the latter internalizes them and turns them into symbols that rouse the sympathetic imagination.

With neither commerce nor sleep available to him, Dickens in "Night Walks" takes to the London streets to find some "companionship" and, eventually, some sleep. But while one society rests, another emerges to the nightwalker, a society that reaches him through dreamlike distortions that carry with them their own unique truths, including the possible truth of his own identity:

> When a church clock strikes, on houseless ears in the dead of the night, it may be at first mistaken for company and hailed as such. But, as the spreading circles of vibration, which you may perceive at such a time with great clearness, go opening out, for ever and ever afterwards widening perhaps (as the philosopher has suggested) in eternal space, the mistake is rectified and the sense of loneliness is profounder. Once—it was after leaving the Abbey and turning my face north—I came to the great steps of St. Martin's church as the clock was striking Three. Suddenly, a thing that in a moment more I should have trodden upon without seeing, rose up at my feet with a cry of loneliness and houselessness, struck out of it by the bell, the like of which I never heard. We then stood face to face looking at one another, frightened by one another. The creature was like a beetle-browed hair-lipped youth of twenty, and it had a loose bundle of rags on, which it held together with one of its hands. It shivered from head to foot, and its teeth chattered, and as it stared at me—persecutor, devil, ghost, whatever it thought me—it made with its whiny mouth as if it were snapping at me, like a worried dog. Intending to give this ugly object money, I put out my hand to stay it—for it recoiled as it whined and snapped—and laid my hand upon its shoulder. Instantly, it twisted out of its garment, like the young man in the New Testament, and left me standing alone with its rags in my hands.[†]

Dickens in this essay has christened himself "Houselessness," which is what characterizes the being he encounters here. Perhaps to be without a house is to become a "thing." "My principal object being to get through the night, the pursuit of it brought me into sympathetic relations with people who have no other object every night in the year."[†] The walk produces strange sympathies, this one a sympathy between atomized units. The entire paragraph is about the illusion of companionship. First the church bell betrays his hopes by making him aware of the endless space through which its sound flows and thereby of his isolation within this endlessness. The creature ultimately evokes the same response. Never described as human, he nonetheless becomes a mirror of Dickens himself, staring face to face, lonely and houseless. The creature seems to consider him a ghost, but it is probably the reverse, that Dickens finds the creature the spectral one. Reaching out to the creature, he is left only with rags. The human encounter has proven to be the most insubstantial.

The grimness of this encounter is undeniable, yet it would be wrong to make it represent the tone or the purpose of the whole essay. This is, after all, a walking essay, which means that no single event of the walk is allowed to convey the experience of the walk in its entirety. This night-walker reminds us of the rural day walker in that he manages, in the midst of his sudden naked encounters, to wrap himself, paradoxically, in his own sheltering reverie, to walk and observe, as he says, "under a kind of fascination."[†] Most of the objects or characters he passes by occasion his own meditations upon them. There is time and distance for thought and imagination, which grant him visions of tragedy, comedy, the grotesque. The everyday "Houselessness" in the walker ceases to be a painful loneliness and, in quiet transformation, becomes a special pleasure: "And it is not, as I used to think, going home at such times, the least wonderful thing in London, that in the real desert region of the night, the houseless wanderer is alone there."[†] Later in the century, in James Thomson's powerful but depressing walking poem, "The City of Dreadful Night," the imagination has no power to extricate itself from the dismal visions of urban corruption. The city's disease infects the walker with a sense of hopelessness:

> No time abates the first despair and awe,
>   But wonder ceases soon; the wierdest thing
> Is felt least strange beneath the lawless law
>   Where Death-in-Life is the eternal king;
> Crushed impotent beneath this reign of terror,
> Dazed with such mysteries of woe and error,
>   The soil is too outward for wondering.[†]

In Dickens the soul still wonders and still manages to recover enough of itself to be fascinated.

I know of two night-walk essays in which the imagination of the walker insinuates itself into the private lives of sleeping citizens. The first, written by Leigh Hunt, draws back from its Peeping Tom impulse, implying that its author would rather experience the city night by distance ruralized. For what really touches him is the tranquillity of the late-hour walk, a journey through a human aether but without human disturbance: "Inanimate objects are no calmer than passions and cares now seem to be, all laid asleep. The human being is motionless as the house or the tree; sorrow is suspended; and you endeavor to think that only love is awake."† But soon he begins to imagine the apothecary who may at any moment be awakened for his services: "I see him now, the pale blinker suppressing the conscious injustice of his anger at being roused by the apprentice, and fumbling himself out of the house, in hoarseness and great-coat, resolved to make the sweetness of the Christmas bill indemnify him for the bitterness of the moment." It is this that rouses the internal censor of his imagination: "But we shall be getting too much into the interior of the houses."† At this point he pushes his way (past one last persistent dog) further into a nocturnal reverie, and as he sinks deeper into dreamy thoughts, he moves further from the city and into the country and closer to home. He encounters watchmen on the way who familiarize the landscape and encourage an undisturbed flow of thought. At one point Hunt confers upon the reader the status of "never-to-be-forgotten and ethereal companion,"† and we too help in our walk through the essay to contribute to its sheltered harmony.

The city, it seems, encourages the imagination to penetrate into it; it encourages the arousal and exercise of a sympathetic, social consciousness. Hunt (and the "ruralizing" imagination) draws back from the city's encouragement. Dylan Thomas, by contrast, yields to it:

> The town was not yet awake, and I walked through the streets like a stranger come out of the sea, shrugging off weed and wave and darkness with each step, or like an inquisitive shadow, determined to miss nothing: not the preliminary tremor in the throat of the dawn-saying cock or the first whirring nudge of arranged time in the belly of the alarm clock on the trinketed chest of drawers under the knitted text and the done-by-hand water colours of Porthcawl or Trinidad.†

His curiosity takes him into the dreams of people, one after another, whose lives during the day appear as tranquil as they do at night but whose dreams and fantasies emerge to him in color, comedy, and pathos. They are more "alive" in their dreams that he has sympathetically revealed through the darkness than they are in the drab day which assumes its relentless tyranny over their lives and forces the short essay to an end:

> Thus some of the voices of a cliff-perched town at the far end of Wales moved out of sleep and darkness into the newborn, ancient and ageless morning, moved and were lost.[†]

This is a pleasurable kind of social consciousness to exercise. Because it relies not on observation but on fantasy, it is more "poetic" than true, and yet the walker is able to accord people a genuine dignity even if it is only the dignity of the dream life.

In Virginia Woolf's beautiful "Street Haunting," hardly has the walk begun and she is, in the manner of Hunt and Thomas, imagining the life in a drawing room that she passes, when she checks herself and withdraws into the chaste pleasure of the eye:

> But here we must stop peremptorily. We are in danger of digging deeper than the eye approves; we are impeding our passage down the smooth stream by catching at some branch or root. At any moment, the sleeping army may stir itself and wake in us a thousand violins and trumpets in response; the army of human beings may arouse itself and assert all its oddities and sufferings and sordidities. Let us dally a little long, be content still with surfaces only.[†]

She avoids being "roused" a little longer; when she finally is roused by human beings on the walk, she never lets their condition overwhelm her. The walk always takes precedence.

Woolf describes how the night walk lulls one into such reveries "when, suddenly, turning the corner, we come upon a bearded Jew, wild, hunger-bitten, glaring out of his misery; or pass the humped body of an old woman flung abandoned on the step of a public building with a cloak over her like the hasty covering thrown over a dead horse or donkey. At such sights the nerves of the spine seem to stand erect; a sudden flare is brandished in our eyes; a question is asked which is never answered."[†] A walker, it appears, does not answer questions because she is an attenuated human identity, an attenuated mind. Instead, when one walks out of one's house, "the shell-like covering which our souls have excreted to house themselves, to make for themselves a shape distinct from others, is broken, and there is left of all these wrinkles and roughnesses a central oyster of perceptiveness, an enormous eye."[†] A walker loses one identity, that defined by complex historical-social existence, but may gain another. Woolf writes in the tradition of William Hazlitt ("On Going a Journey"), who enjoyed the anonymity of trampers and who walked to "be oneself again." As she walks, the oyster of perceptiveness transforms itself into a free imagination, more intent upon its own activity than upon discovering "answers" to the world. When Nature

> set about her masterpiece, the making of man, she should have thought of one thing only. Instead, turning her head, looking over her shoulder, into each one of us she let creep instincts and desires which are utterly at variance with his main being, so that we are streaked, variegated, all of a mixture; the colours have run. Is the true self this which stands on the pavement in January, or that which bends over the balcony in June? Am I here, or am I there? Or is the true self neither this or that, neither here nor there, but something so varied and wandering that it is only when we give the rein to its wishes and let it take its way unimpeded that we are indeed ourselves?"[†]

This passage brings her to the limit of unimpeded inner life. There is fear in the undefined, and she is glad to reach a secondhand bookshop and "find anchorage in the thwarting currents of being" among the books, any one of which may "turn into the best friend we have in the world." A walker can identify with secondhand books, "wild books, homeless books." Indeed it is comforting here, after experiencing such an excessive flowing out of oneself into imagination, to read about travelers in books: "This packing up and going off, exploring deserts and catching fevers, settling in India for a lifetime, penetration even to China. . . ." There is a comfort in the written, no matter what the subject is; the latter part of her essay, concerned with comfort, shelter, and the recovery of a familiar unity of being, is also concerned with books, stories, dramas, and, finally, a pencil, which had been the "excuse" for her journey and which she brings home as 'the only spoil' from the city.[†] The tone of the essay (indeed of all her essays) has a "literary" comfort, a lyrical pleasure with what could be the very nonlyrical subjects of a night walk in London (in fact, it is actually an "evening" walk). Or perhaps the appropriate literary model is drama rather than lyric: "Into each of these lives one could penetrate a little way, far enough to give oneself the illusion that one is not tethered to a single mind, but can put on briefly the bodies and minds of others "[†] The walk here and the walking essay are a kind of game, a playing at sympathy; yet the play itself as play is, of course, very real, and the exercise of the imagination is very real. The city gives forth questions to Woolf, but she does not think that they demand answers.

Leslie Stephen uses Wordsworth to legitimate the ruralizing imagination in London, both for his ability to discover "nature" in the city as well as for his general perspective on the primal relationship between nature and human life. Stephen's essay, "In Praise of Walking," concerns itself largely with rural walking, "recalls better places and nobler forms of the exercise,"[†] namely the country, and he invokes Wordsworth's poor Susan who, standing in the middle of the city, imagines dramatic scenes in nature. Similarly in "London Walks," Stephen assures us on the second page that for the walker there is plenty of nature in London. Stephen is aware, however, that the people of London, who were supposed to prove to Emerson that "the devil was still in full activity," are for him a vast unindividualized hypnotic mass that forms a backdrop for daydreaming superior in this respect to that in the country itself. Paradoxically the ruralization of the city occurs best when people have become most dehumanized: "My fellow-creatures are to my eyes provokingly uniform . . . ." " . . . the race at large is to me a vast collection of automata, which may, it is true, be animated by souls, but, for my purposes, would be equally interesting if worked by springs."[†]

"London Walks" is simply saturated with Wordsworth. The entire essay is bracketed by allusions to the sonnet, "Composed upon Westminster Bridge," a poem written from the perspective of distance, both temporal and spatial, from the dehumanized London of industry, bathing the city in pastoral associations and animating it with personification. Just as Wordsworth finds this London more beautiful than nature, so does Stephen, but both of them must see it in some way distanced: Wordsworth by standing on the bridge before the working day has begun and Stephen through the London fog—"Sentiment begins with mist." Dotting the essays with brief quotations from and allusions to the "Immortality Ode," *The Prelude*, and other touches of Wordsworth, Stephen legitimates the perspective of distance, the ruralizing of the urban reality. The essay begins with a celebration of the power of the eye to transform "the meanest flower that blows" into something of sublime and epic proportions. London becomes a series of largely soothing impressions, mediated by mist, distance, and the ghost of Wordsworth.

At one point Stephen imagines a novelist who could tell the individual stories of all those "atoms" of persons whom he passes by on his London walk, a writer of such stature that he could "succeed in piercing to the heart of this monstrous concretion, and compressing into a few pages the pith and essence of the thoughts of which the ordinary wayfarer through its streets catches at intervals by the extreme skirts or fringes."[†] It is strange that he had to imagine such a novelist, who, in fact, already existed—Dickens, Gaskill, Gissing, Zola. But even Dickens (who wrote a tongue-in-cheek walking essay called "Arcadian London") saves the nightmares for characters in his novels and while passing them by, sheltered in his passage, finds pleasure in scenes that, were he to stop, would fill him with distress.

11.

The Urban Walker

I. A Man and His Dog

In a humorous Kertesz photograph a man drags his reluctant dog across a snowy New York City street. This dog may still be this man's best friend, but at the moment it does not add to the man's pleasure on the walk. Usually the dog is either an antenna for approaching intrusion and interruption or fulfills in body the mental errancy of the walker. As the mind dips in and out of some topic, the dog scurries after a squirrel behind a tree, sniffing out a line on the ground, doubling back through bushes and dead branches, stopping and pointing at a bird's call, heading off again as the bird fails to materialize; it tears ahead of its master, returns, lags far behind, and returns again. The dog forms an image of the mental walk that all walkers add to their journey along the street or path.

Hazlitt argued strenuously that one should walk alone. But the dog is the perfect compromise between the severity of solitude and the clutter of companionship, put positively the freedom of one and the comfort of the other. Without inhibiting one's thoughts, it comforts the walker in his solitude by mirroring his activities; and like the image in a mirror, the dog requires the human walker for its own continued motions. A person and a dog compose an idyll of walking.

Thomas Mann's "A Man and His Dog" ("Herr und Hund") is a long, modern idyll of life seen through the eyes of the author-as-walker and his dog Bashan. Several of Mann's best stories—"A Weary Hour," "Death in Venice," "Disorder and Early Sorrow"—follow the prescription of the idyll, that the wishes and fantasies of the person eek out a narrow but decisive victory over the forces of the world. The so-called narrative of historical present for which Mann is well-known places at the foreground of our attention the walk of the hero's thoughts and associations, but no story exploits this technique more lovingly than "A Man and His Dog." All energy, at times joyful, ferocious, stupid, faithful, the dog circles around the author as he moves even-paced—the concretizing of fantasy life into a natural form, as if fantasy had recurred to a seasonal existence. Although it alludes at the beginning to Schubert's *Unfinished Symphony* ("two notes, tonic and lower fourth . . . might be considered the musical setting of a two-syllable name"),[†] this work seems modeled on Beethoven's *Pastoral Symphony*, with is programmatic movements based upon changes in weather and mood.

Mann's walking idyll belongs strictly neither to country or to city, but to the suburbs. It may be that the idyll itself is the literary source for modern suburban thought and planning since it envisions life as not only comic but also protected. For Goethe and Schiller, Mann's illustrious predecessors in this genre, in both practice and theory, suburbia may seem far from the philosophical idealisms they envisioned. And yet the conjunction of landscape and technology serving pleasure and security found in *Elective Affinities* and implicitly in *Faust*, Part II, makes the association to suburbia less strange. They did not anticipate that the lure of the idyll would lead to a technology designed to tame or disarm the unconscious and designed to falsify the needs and rights of those not in power. Suburbia makes difference not real.

Mann's suburban idyll lies somewhere between the original vision of freedom and mental play and its modern antiseptic manifestations.

The oldest literary rendering of the suburbs that I know of is the *Aeneid*, Book II. Aeneas wakes up in his father's house in the suburbs of Troy to the sounds of the fighting between the Greeks and his fellow Trojan citizens. Bewildered, as in a nightmare, he walks through the city amidst the fighting to its center, only to witness at last the beheading of Priam and the final desecration of the palace and what that means, the end of Trojan civilization. The suburbs are the place where the symbols and the forces of civilization are not in clear focus. For Aeneas the walk to the center of the city makes the images and conflicts of Troy sharp and real.

On their walk Thomas Mann and Bashan "re-create" the suburban unconscious. The famous writer does not take his dog to his work in the city. Instead they often walk near a riverbank and through a section of suburban planning that was never completed, a real-estate enterprise for which the plans exceeded the financial resources for carrying them out (an allusion to German financial losses during World War I?). There are plenty of signs of the activity of the project: dykes by the river, gardens, and the layout of streets. Mann likes above all the system of street signs based on famous figures of German and European civilization— like Adalbert-Stifterstrasse:

> They have not been kept up or renewed, the climate has done its worst by them. The enamel has scaled off, the lettering is rusty, there are ugly broken-edged gaps which make the names sometimes almost illegible. One of them, indeed, puzzled me a good deal when I first came here and was spying about the neighbourhood. It was a long name, and the word "street' was perfectly clear, but most of the rest was eaten by rust; there remained only an S at the beginning, a E somewhere about the middle, and another E at the end. I could not reckon with so many unknown quantities. I studied the sign a long time with my hands behind my back, then continued along the foot-path with Bashan. I thought I was thinking about something else, but all the time my brains were privately cudgelling themselves, and suddenly it came over me. I stopped with a start, stood still, and then hastened back, took up my former position, and tested my guess. Yes, it fitted. The name on the street where I was walking was Shakespeare Street.[†]

The dog, in its own way, partakes of this project in cultural archaeology. But it also grants to Mann's walk the exercise of an archaic, aggressive unconscious. It loves to hunt, to chase birds, rabbits, mice, even deer. Mann only watches—the silent pact between them—lending Bashan his "moral support" and registering to himself the full range of feelings unleashed by the dog's carnal urges. Should he help Bashan trap the rabbit or unearth the mouse? He wavers intensely between his own sympathies and urges and his sense of human decorum, now a finely tuned protagonist in one of the greatest of all modern walking idylls.

II. Sidewalks and Streets

"A city sidewalk by itself is nothing. It is an abstraction. . . . The same might be said of streets, . . . "[†] Later on, in the same brilliant work by Jane Jacobs, *The Death and Life of Great American Cities*, she says: "A city cannot be a work of art."[†] Although separated by 350 pages, the two comments seem to be mutually reinforcing. A sidewalk ideally exists as an instrument of passage, an occasion for conversation and commerce, an occasion for play. It occasions the true life of citizens—getting and spending, but also regulating with a kind of moral intuition the safety of the neighborhood. A sidewalk built with beauty in mind usually neglects these functions or at least interprets the desired human experience differently. In Lewis Mumford's many studies of city planning, aesthetic considerations, particularly notions of country beauty, dominate. Cities need the beauty of the country infused into them to give joy to the person embedded in the sinister urban realities. Interestingly, for Mumford, the person who registers the success of city planning is the pedestrian. For Jacobs walking is only one of many primary activities. Mumford's walker lives for visual pleasure; his experience of pleasure is solitary, just as it is for the country walker. The model for this walker surely is the rural perambulators of the nineteenth century. Jacobs's sidewalk citizens presumably experience the intimate pleasure of solitary walking but only as a by-product of living the human-faceted neighborhood life. This kind of intimacy, on Jacobs's neighborhood sidewalk is not advertised or projected. Here intimacy is not the point though the sidewalk does not spurn those who walk that way.

Curiously and touchingly, when she is moved to sum up what she considers the integrated and self-sustaining unit of a healthy urban neighborhood, Jacobs resorts to a metaphor of aesthetic movement, "the heart-of-the-day ballet":

> Under the seeming disorder of the old city, wherever the old city is working successfully, is a marvelous order for maintaining the safety of the streets and

the freedom of the city. . . . This order is all composed of movement and change, and although it is life, not art, we may fancifully call it the art form of the city and liken it to the dance—not to a simpleminded precision dance with everyone kicking up at the same time, twirling in unison and bowing off en masse, but to an intricate ballet in which the individual dancers and ensembles all have distinctive parts which miraculously reinforce each other and compose an orderly whole. The ballet of the good city sidewalk never repeats itself from place to place, and in any one place is always replete with new improvisations.[†]

Why does Jacobs, resolutely set against the aestheticizing of the city, fancy the neighborhood in such a metaphor? Because she finds the innate capacity for neighborhood self-regulation, the civic impulse, so to speak, a beautiful thing. But to develop a street or sidewalk under the category of "the beautiful"—which usually implies something about its shape, its proximity to trees and flowers and grass, its distance from automobile traffic—is to impose a Romantic ideology on a human activity and necessarily to oversimplify and finally to destroy the complex civic organism.

From the Romantic point of view the modern city is the site of isolation and alienation. From Jacobs's, the city can be—and is occasionally—the site of civic life in the best sense. Viewing Giacometti's "Groupe 3 Hommes II," stimulates in me both perspectives. Each figure walks purposively away from the other two; the group suggests centrifugal, dispersing movement from a center. No one notices the others. Two are passing each other while the third has already moved beyond the group into (from the observer's perspective) more pronounced separateness. The torsos of all three leaning forward and the heads erect increase the sense that energy and mind are directed into the distance and the future. It is easy to interpret this group in terms of the atomization of modern life: people physically in proximity yet mentally and emotionally caught up in their private bubbles of need and desire. But this composition to me feels more like Jacobs's ballet. It does not communicate loneliness and pain or numbness. For all the spareness and distinctness of the figures, the composition as a whole simply reports on the fine, if various, business of city life.

In Kertesz's photographs the walker and the sidewalk and street compose a dream of city life. Looking down a broad Parisian sidewalk and a treelined street (a bicyclist barely visible against the trees), I own the empty sidewalk with my eye: I am the only walker.

By contrast, Kertesz's Hungarian contemporary, Brassaï's "Paris Street at Night" (1932), also looks down a long sidewalk, but there is no comfort, no sense of ownership or mastery. The narrow sidewalk is flanked by building fronts and black automobiles; the scene is dark but lit by blazing streetlamps the gleam from which drowns in the fierce darkness. The empty sidewalk comes toward me menacingly. I can hear my own hollow footsteps.

If a streetwalker appears at the corner of a street lit in the same ragged glow as in another Brassai photograph from 1932, the discomfort remains in the emptiness but loses its menacing aspect: wrapped in a dark cloak, the lust she carries is nearly hidden.

The walkers on Kertesz's streets and sidewalks do not belong to Jane Jacobs's world of neighborhoods. They are ciphers of my nostalgia and wish. Often the sidewalk or street has more texture and motion and striking shape than does the moving walker. The curve of a street corner or a square or plaza, often photographed from above, subsume to themselves the activity of the work and the imagination of the viewer. As I project myself onto his wide, accessible sidewalks, I never imagine myself talking with another—only walking and looking, nourished by the pavement into the fine reverie.

I look down from my Parisian apartment onto the "Pont Neuf on a Rainy Morning" (1931) to see wide cobblestone streets at the corner empty of traffic and of all activity except for three walkers heading somewhere quickly through the rain. This is a cozy perspective as, I think, it would be for me were I out walking. With Kertesz I conflate my viewer's imagination with that of the walker.

Curbs are traditionally dangerous, unsanitary places. One can get splashed or hit. But Kertesz ("Sidewalk," 1929) turns the curb into abstract art. A close-up from above yields three vertical strips and textures: 1) long, smooth stones on the sidewalk; 2) water flowing like lava down a shallow gutter; 3) cobblestones in the street at right angles to the stones of the sidewalk. In another photograph two cocks face each other—one in the street and the other on the curb. In both works the clashing, alien activities of street and sidewalk neutralize in aesthetic balance and design.

The famous Washington Square photographs from the 1950s recall the valued wavy lines of eighteenth-century English gardens and parks. The snow paths in the square curving endlessly past empty park benches, curving fences, and elegantly drooping park lamps and the tiny black walkers bundled in coats together become an emblem of the walker's bundled-up reveries. These are snow-white reveries veined with a tracery of bare trees. In one of this series the park lamps are lit at night. The eye searches in vain for the walker. One follows the swirls of walks, fences, a frozen pond. Ah! there are some footsteps in the snow. Ah! there are more! And soon I will add mine to these in the silent language of solitary winter walkers.

III. The Walker and the Crowd

One viewer of Kertesz has observed that he makes our " troublesome" metropolis seem "intimate, loveable." While this is obviously true, there are moments when that transformation seems to reflect a wish to make modern cities and their crowds vanish, or to be the one who vanishes, or at least to be the one whose sublunary legs vanish. In 1984, the year before his death, Kertesz went back to his native Hungary and photographed the villages after a lifetime of the troublesome metropolises of Paris and New York. Of the two photographs called "Hungary August 11, 1984" that I have seen, one shows a village lane filled with cows. The other eschews the ground and the path altogether. A stork sits on a massive nest that it has built on a thatched rooftop of a house only suggested. Its head thrown back and bill open, the bird calls upward and outward to an unseen mate against the background of sky and cloud. Or does it call to the cloud itself? The photograph is about the final relief from loneliness, the human wish for such joyous relief pictured as nature itself. In literature it reminds me of the vision of the ancient mariner:

> In his loneliness and fixedness he yearneth towards the journeying Moon, and the stars that still sojourn, yet still move onward; and every where the blue sky belongs to them, and is their appointed rest, and their native coun-

André Kertesz, "Washington Square, Winter, 1954," photograph. Courtesy of the Estate of André Kertesz.

André Kertesz, "Pont Neuf, Paris, 1931," photograph. Courtesy of the Estate of
André Kertesz.

try and their own natural homes, which they enter unannounced, as lords that are certainly expected and yet there is a silent joy at their arrival.[†]

From this perspective Kertesz's walkers, like the ancient mariner, carry within them a vision of joy that alienates them from their present reality, a utopia that subverts the pleasure and vitality of the walk. In photographing those graceful sidewalk curves, Kertesz imagines that chaste heaven of clouds, nests, and winged calls.

How different from this is Poe's and Baudelaire's suspicion-filled hunger for the crowds of London and Paris! Unwilling to forego either that heaven of imagination or the power of drives and unwilling to deny the poetry of the solitary or the fact of membership in the urban community, Baudelaire walks through the streets driven and sad, excited at once by the power of anonymous urban bodies and the thought of their sad, beautiful souls.

> The pleasure of being in crowds is a mysterious expression of sensual joy in the multiplication of Number.[†]

> Sexuality is the lyricism of the masses.[†]

Baudelaire walking through crowds has this particular pleasure: " . . . this divine prostitution of the soul giving itself entire, all its poetry and all its charity, to the unexpected as it comes along, to the stranger as he passes".[†]

> What oddities one finds in big cities when one knows how to roam and to look! Life swarms with innocent monsters.[†]

As the poet climbs a hill, he looks down upon the cities and sees its objects: "Monstrosities flowering like a flower."

> . . . just now as I was crossing the boulevard in a great hurry, splashing through the mud in the midst of a seething chaos, and with death galloping at me from every side, I gave a sudden start and my halo slipped off my head and fell into the mire of the macadam. I was far too frightened to pick it up. I decided it was less unpleasant to lose my insignia than to get my bones broken. Then too, I reflected, every cloud has its silver lining. I can now go

about incognito, be as low as I please and indulge in debauch like ordinary mortals.[†]

Baudelaire's presence in the crowd creates the contradictions that he feels as alienating, perverse, extravagant. He is always the foreign element. He makes himself foreign by "taking a bath of multitude," by forcing his experience of intimacy upon a world that denies it:

> enjoying a crowd is an art; and only he can relish a debauch of vitality at the expense of the human species, on whom, in his cradle, a fairy has bestowed the love of masks and masquerading, the hate of home, and the passion for roaming.[†]

Does this poet of the cities do anything fundamentally different from the rural idealists from Wordsworth to Kertesz? Baudelaire shows what happens when the Romantic walker/poet loses his halo. The city takes it from him. He discovers that his halo, his mark as an individual, with a utopianizing soul, was more a burden than a consolation and a strength. Yet the ideology of souls and beauty does not leave him. No one around him cares as he slips in the mud and enjoys it except, perhaps, those of similar "superior" cast who may walk like him and who will read him: mon semblable! mon frère!

Baudelaire sees the new urban crowd as thoroughly unknowable. Eventually focusing on one person, he finds his own mournful alienation: the poor widow listening, in the mob, to some beautiful music of the aristocracy; or the old clown who, in a crowd of holiday revellers appears sad and beaten. The poet wants to give him money but is swept away by the relentless wave of the crowd; himself beaten, he reflects at once on himself and the clown, who is like the poet living beyond the generation of customers delighted with his tricks. He seeks out beauty and finds it alternately repulsive and melancholy but (like Wordsworth encountering the blind beggar in the crowds of London) also finds it apocalyptic, something that he imagines affirms his being and design beyond the categories of the crowd, of time and history.

The crowd has a deafening roar. Like a swollen river or the ocean itself, the visible movement of the crowd registers the powerful, irrational energies that move it. For Gustave Le Bon in the last century, "the substitution of the unconscious action of crowds for the conscious activity of individuals is one of the principle characteristics of the present age."† For the generations leading up to Freud, the crowd was the manifestation of the unconscious life in society. Le Bon proposes that the crowd is primarily dangerous when it is not understood—like the early Freudian unconscious—and suppressed. But "is it not the genius of crowds that has furnished the thousands of grains of dust forming the soil in which they have sprung up."† Let us recognize that genius and the individual, soul intact and with a vision formed in heaven, stands in crucial relation to the crowd, just as the creative artist—in the early Freudian view—taps into his powerful unconscious generous to serve, in order to break past the uncreative and predictable regidities of the conscious mind.

"Why should I drive my body from place to place, when my soul travels so lightly?"† The answer to Baudelaire's question (in *Paris Spleen*) lies in the meaning and lure of the crowd. The crowd is sexuality itself, the unconscious drive. The poet elbows his way through to lose himself in debauchery and dismember the conscious mind, to disinherit it. Yet this, of course, never completely happens since Baudelaire—like Le Bon—retains his faith in the visionary poetry of the individual. So the poet who falls on his face in the street's mud still is the poet of the skies, an identification actually certified by his ignominious fall.

Poe's *The Man of the Crowd*, translated admiringly by Baudelaire, is an erotically triangular tale about a walker/poet, the man of the crowd, and the crowd itself. Convalescing from an illness, the poet sits at the window of a hotel restaurant observing the crowds on the sidewalks. One old man, looking as feverish as the poet feels, catches his attention to the extent that he leaves the hotel in curious pursuit, which goes on through the night and throughout the city of London until the next morning. Finally the poet gives up the search to discover the intention, apparently evil, of the old man when he realizes that he can identify him as "the man of the crowd," one who will never reveal himself as an individual, who belongs irrevocably to the crowd and carries with him to the grave a secret that "can never be read." The poet may be said to lose the man of the crowd to the crowd itself, to lose the competition with this black otherness. In this story the crowd is a distorted and perverted humanity (as Walter Benjamin points out); nobody good or generous or creative or valuable belongs to it or comes from it. No individual springs from it—as in Wordsworth or Baudelaire—mournful but beautiful. Thus the crowd like its man keeps the walker/poet, in spite of his night-long wanderings, chaste and confirmed in his comfortable separateness from the crowd. In the world of Poe's story the crowd and its inhabitants cannot be known; they are truly the unconscious if not the unnamable. As the fever of the poet passes, as he convalesces, he resumes his cool distance from the lure of the sidewalk.

IV. The Peripatetic Philosopher

. . . the truth is, that at no time of my life have I been a person to hold myself polluted by the touch or approach of any creature that wore a human shape: on the contrary, from my very earliest youth it has been my pride to converse familiarly, *more Socratico*, with all human beings, man, woman, and child, that chance might fling in my way: a practice which is friendly to the knowledge of human nature, to good feelings, and to that frankness of address which becomes a man who would be thought a philosopher. For a philosopher should not see with the eyes of the poor limitary creature calling himself a man of the world, and filled with narrow and self-regarding prejudices of birth and education, but should look upon himself as a catholic creature and as standing in an equal relation to high and low—to educated and unedu-cated, to the guilty and the innocent. Being myself at that time of necessity a peripatetic, or a walker of the streets, I naturally fell in more frequently with those female peripatetics who are technically called street-walkers.[†]

De Quincey's prostitutes (unlike Brassaï's on the street corner) emit no erotic excitement. For most of his *Confessions*, De Quincey protests that poverty and isolation have hurled him into the crowd unwillingly. At the same time he declares himself a peripatetic philosopher, i.e., one who is drawn to the varieties of the crowd out of a Romantic conviction in the value—for poets and philosophers—of *disinterestedness*. Without any par-ticular prejudice or partisan view, he observes simply in order to know and therefore remains separate and untouched. He is at once touched and untouched, perhaps the inevitable condition of the walker. Ann, the orphan who saves him from his weakness from hunger and is later lost to him, becomes the exception to his disinterested state. His plea-sure in an opiated perambulation through the neighborhoods of London's poor on a Saturday night becomes, in his search for Ann, "pursued through many a year in dreams." The pleasure reverts to a paranoid design: "The general idea of a search and a chase reproduced itself in many shapes."†

Poe, De Quincey, and Baudelaire: all walkers unable or unwilling to know the man or woman of the crowd. Yet this unknowability becomes a pleasure and a beauty:

> The true object in my *Opium Confessions* is not the naked physiological theme— on the contrary, *that* is the ugly pole, the murderous spear, the halbert— but those wandering musical variations upon the theme, those parasitical thoughts, feelings, digressions, which climb up with bells and blossoms round about the arid stock; ramble away from it at times with perhaps too rank a luxuriance; but at the same time, by the eternal interest attached to the *subjects* of these digressions, no matter what were the execution, spread a glory over incidents that for themselves would be—less than nothing.†

Benjamin calls the "glory spread over incidents" an aura, that distancing obscurity because of which the viewer, or walker, finds his own need for self confirmation in the world ratified in the beautiful. The reality remains arid and ugly. It is easier to respond to evil than to ugliness or to what appears to be disgusting. Evil simply perverts the good but still speaks in its language. The ugly is different; it refuse that language and its assumption altogether, threatens the person who reacts by casting it out of the "heaven" of the familiar and consoling into the "hell" of the disgusting. Perhaps this helps to explain De Quincey's racism in the *Confessions* and *Suspiria*, the condescension toward Orientals and Asians. The language of the walk reinforces the language of art: the prose of his thoughts, feelings, and digressions will "ramble" away from the naked physiological (and, we might add, social) theme, to the point that our interest in the walk itself will overwhelm our interest in the reality. The walk becomes the seductive tangle of language, erotized permanently like the life in search of Ann and deepened in its welcoming obscurity by opium.

Usually we distinguish between the country walk and the city walk, but De Quincey's Confessions shows how fragile, how illusory at times, this distinction is. For the twin aspiration—along with the recovery of

Ann the prostitute—is the journey to the Lake District, to Grasmere and Wordsworth, the poet of the consoling and visionary walk through nature. Although, as a peripatetic philosopher, De Quincey has claimed his affinity for urban encounters, they seem in fact to reinforce his solitude. They draw him back to his opium and his dreams, Ann and the mild nature of the north, and to his "parasitical" prose. Walking becomes a metaphor for reveries, wandering thought. Does this take the walking dreamer deeper into himself? This is not at all clear, but probably De Quincey's walk begins with exploration—continued by Poe, Baudelaire, then Nerval and the Surrealists—of the power of the city upon the imaginations of those who find the city inimical to the individual life. Paradoxically both the city (the enemy) and the individual seem enhanced by the connection. The political nature of the dreaming mind gets established. The lure of an urban life that simultaneously repels, the visionary ecstasy that accompanies the ugliness and poverty of urban scenes, the mournful beauty of the woman sought or envisioned, all speak to the welcomed contradictions of the urban Romantic walker. Wordsworth's poor Susan is probably a London streetwalker, enchanted by the note of a bird hanging like herself in the same spot. Trapped by the bad city, she envisions her idyllic release. But perhaps the reveries belong to the poet, himself walking through the city and beyond the "deafening street" of the crowd entering or creating the saving imagination of the poor girl. Susan's bad life can be documented; the poet documents his response to it. The walker, alienated from the city, can, through his alienation and visionary imagination, still describe in beauty one of its mournful casualties.

From De Quincey and even more from Baudelaire the emphasis lies upon the walker's mental "rambles," extravagances and contortions. Walter Benjamin says of Baudelaire's sonnet "A une passante": "Far from experiencing the crowd as an opposed, antagonistic element, this very crowd brings to the city dweller the figure that fascinates. The delight of the urban poet is love—not at first sight, but at last sight. It is a farewell forever that coincides in the poem with the moment of enchantment. . . . What makes his body contract in a tremor [at seeing a passing, tall, majestic woman in mourning]—*crispe comme un extravagant*, Baudelaire says—is not the rapture of a man whose every fiber is suffused with *eros*; it is, rather, like the kind of sexual shock that can beset a lonely man . . . "

> A lightning flash . . . then night!—O fleeting beauty
> Whose glance all of a sudden gave me new birth,
> Shall I see you again only in eternity?
>
> Far, far from here! Too late! or maybe, *never?*
> For I know not where you flee, you know not where I go,
> O you I would have loved (O you who knew it too!)" †

No crowd flows or roars by in Blake's London. Yet the city seems heavily populated. Blake observes many people just as Poe does from his hotel restaurant window. For Baudelaire the crowd would be the site of human anonymity from which would emerge the face of mournful love. In that face he finds the sadness of the lost individual, the sadness of himself. His poem ends in the language of possible love, but its conditional grammar fixes it forever as a rigid fact of the walker's utopian dream: "O you I would have loved (o you who knew it too!)." The poet's empathy is only an idea. Blake's empathy enters and fastens upon the members of the crowd itself: " . . . mark in every face I meet / marks of weakness, marks of woe."† The fine play on the work "mark" is the sign of empathy, for the act of noticing or perceiving is the act of inscribing the perception; and the perception and the inscription become, in their identity with the stigmata of oppression, the empathetic transference of oppression to the freer space of prophetic poetry.

Blake's walker begins in freedom. He wanders, that is, embraces the city and its crowds with a gesture that defies the chartering hand of authority. Yet his freedom does not insulate him from the utterances of human life. His freedom, in fact, allows him to hear those utterances and mark their abnormality. He becomes astonishingly receptive, able to register the sight or sound and its meaning or cause simultaneously. This is the mental part of his wandering, not the Rousseauian reveries of self-absorption and congratulation, but an openness to what is planned to be a carefully hidden connection between the sights and sounds of urban life and their sinister origins behind the walls of ecclesiastical and regal power.

He hears the cry of the sweep and the infant and the sigh of the soldier, but nobody else does. These sounds never reach those whose minds are manacled. This is the individuality of the anonymous member of the crowd: his utterances are intercepted by and reify upon the walls of oppression, like notches in a gunman's belt.

Blake's walker, who marks this hideous phenomenon, may be the first surrealist.

In the nineteenth century and still at times in the twentieth, the walker becomes vulnerable to a shock. Seemingly at one with the crowd, dulled by the numbers, he nonetheless receives the jolt of electricity when the vision of beauty-as-longing-for-companionship reaches him. But the people in the city, the city itself, have learned to absorb the shocks with infinite quickness, dwarf the losses:

> On Brooklyn Bridge I saw a man drop dead.
> It meant no more than if he were a sparrow.
>
> Above us rose Manhattan;
> below, the river spread to meet the sky.[†]

This poet marks his consciousness of being invulnerable, being of the membership of the unconscious, the anonymous. This is the voice of the city and the crowd.

12.

Journey Through a Degas Exhibit, Metropolitan Museum of Art, New York

1. I've just completed my tour of the second room after having left the first, laden particularly with a memory of a tiny etching of Dante meeting Vergil, among a swarm of early portraits and self-portraits. Dante and Vergil have come on one another in their own journeys. Vergil's walk through centuries has been from one symbolic representation of himself to another. Now he presents himself to Dante and to us without our seeing his previous steps. He is still, like a picture on the wall (I wrote mistakenly "walk") that begins to talk as one brings one's own steps to it. Dante's cloudy darkness of his lost life illuminates Vergil. For Dante has the illusion that Vergil is still, that his paces have stopped and in the stopping have transfigured him. Yet as they talk and walk together, descending and then ascending, Vergil will become a Psyche, lost yet found by his Cupid Dante. Vergil becomes the feminine Beatrice by this walk through the images of sin and purgation. There descent and ascent measure a gradient of transformations. I'm remembering all this from gallery two. I've stopped, seated on a bench in the center of the room, my pen walking for me, both in relief, to assuage the searing disappointment of walking by one picture for the next. For this passus on the page requires leaving nothing behind. It is always a filling, an early autumnal event. The fruit grows, I hope toward ripeness, the steps slowly climbing to the next landing, wherever that will be.

2. As I've been writing this last paragraph, I've occasionally glanced up to two portraits in this room, or rather, my eye walks back and forth between them—what a strategy for continuing the walk without elegizing, grieving the loss of, any painting in my travels. Before me (my eyes have only to stand up—or are they kneeling?) is Yves Gobillard-Morisot, pastel, 1869, in black but the green of nature seen through the window behind her. Her light brunette hair is in twists and curls that plays on her forehead and spiral down her neck behind. (Another walker has momentarily blotted her from view.) The background is so much softer than her well-etched features.

3. In my reverie I have been layering, that is, walking over or through, these impressions with journeys back to the last pictures in gallery one, Corot's *Reverie*, a young peasant woman sitting contentedly, somewhat curved and bowed but full, autumnal, in the world. She graded me into this second room; women are hard to leave, but here beside Yves Gobillard-Morisot is another pastel, this time by Manet, of Madame Valtesse de la Bigne, with blond hair and blue dress and sharp facial features and bust, no background but light grey shadow and white. She is Psyche for this room; in fact, it is Psyche I approach and pass in all of these beautiful portraits (not only female but male, such as Degas's etching of Manet sitting with a kind of genius of awkwardness on a spindly chair). Who is Psyche, after all, but (for Heine and Kafka, at least) the spirit of love we long to possess on our journey and whom we love the more as we walk by them? But my pen has walked long enough and requires my necessarily crude and unsettling steps through the next gallery.

4. I have walked around gallery three once, a room of Degas's dancers. I'm going against my grain by writing at this point because I'm so full and yet energized that I feel like moving on. I can hardly stand the filling walk with the pen, but I'm afraid of losing some valuable impressions. Here there is no where to sit, so I stand in the middle of the room with people walking behind and in front and to the side, my notebook crooked in my hand and forearm. The sign upon entering this room said, "Early Dancers 1871–1881," but I first saw a violinist in pastel and charcoal on green paper. No dancer, or is it he, his head resting on or poised over the head of his burnt red violin playing, bow arm in flight?

THE WALK: NOTES ON A ROMANTIC IMAGE

He is the dancer. But look—he has no bow. My eye walks to the next picture, and there he is again. The bow has leapt into his hands, and a young dancer is intently at work, one foot pointed forward, one hand in support at the bar. Psyche has appeared again on my walk.

I feel heavy in her presence and the rest of them as I walk around the room. But then I remember, "Was man nicht erfliegen kann, muss man erhinken." I limp from dancer to dancer and think of Hephaestos pouring wine amidst the laughter of the gods and the antiphonal sweet songs of the muses.

5. What does it mean, "a dancer who dances," and why do Degas's dancers create that phrase on my walk? "Three dancers preparing for class," "Two dancers" (one tying the other's shoe), "Seated Dancer," "Dancer adjusting Slipper," I walk on and see "Dancers practicing at the bar." "A dancer who dances"—I walk to "who" and the qualification robs her of her defined activity because she sits or ties or balances or prepares or adjusts, but isn't dancing. But then I look again and see her animation and grace in her sitting or adjusting or preparing, and she dances again, closer to me. When we discard Hephaestos's limp, our minds leap and twist into the dance. Is this an etheralized walk, or is the walk a burdened dance?

6. Finally I encounter a barely visible pencil sketch on salmon paper of a lovely soft-haired dancer in soft motion. Here again is Psyche! Before leaving the room I see "Dancers in the Rehearsal Room, with a double base." They dance each in her own character but in a line with the double base bringing up the rear. Their grace pulls the somber old instrument slowly along. In the distance is the dancing class where their walking dance will eventually land them.

7. Unlike Dante I walk around and around in each room, a peasant woman sitting in the fields from morning to night: Corot of two galleries ago. At first the next gallery looks dull after the dancers. Small pictures on the long walls, blacks, and dull browns, and reds dominate. I can walk through here quickly, partly relieved and yet disappointed. But slow down and look more closely; there is time. "Pictures within Pictures," my printed Vergil on the wall tells me. Walking with feet, mind,

pen naturally encourages me toward any doublings. Here is "The Collector of Prints," deep in his black frock coat, black hat, hidden by a burly mustache and beard, yet with strong eyes and prominent lean nose drawing him toward us. A portfolio opens between his knees; it is stuffed with prints. Prints lie overflowing on a table behind him. Behind me, I recall, is a picture of a man with a stuffed bookcase. To my right is a large painting of a painter surrounded by other paintings, some finished and some still easel-bound. There collectors are themselves pictures of contentment, one resting on his knees and looking confidently at us, another with equal confidence looks at us while leaning back in his chair, but the third book collector sits taut and energetic, even aggressively in his chair, his volumes rising potently behind him. For collecting has an aggressive element in it; it is an assertion of power, an imperialistic impulse, perhaps it is unhealthy. Yet who is being subdued? Traveling through the museum I could imagine all these Degases chained to the walls, torn into submission into rows instead of each one separate and dignified standing on some sympathetic lover's wall, in someone's room full of personality and even devotion. And yet together they take on the power of an ideal community; they all strive together, talk to one another. Indeed, perhaps the general buzz of the walkers through the galleries is only an echo of the whispers between the paintings themselves. Pictures within pictures; walks within walks; whispers within whispers. These repetitions are of a finer tone.

As I leave this gallery I encounter an unobtrusive painting that confirms for me the great compassionate power of collecting. It is called "Sulking," a distinguished man sits at his table, head turned down and away, burdened with the mystery. His young wife (or is it his daughter?) stands, leaning on the back of a chair, in his direction yet at a distance from him. At first I thought she was comforting him (because she comforts me), but I think she too is sulking, with him and perhaps because of him. She looks at me, comfortingly? pleasingly? Behind them, just encompassing both heads, is a painting of tremendous vitality, an English racing print called "Steeple Chase Cracks." The horses in full motion suggest powerful sexuality, which perhaps is behind their sulkiness but is perhaps a deep connection between the two. Of the English print the accompanying blurb says: "Its arch of leaping horses effectively links the isolated figures' heads in his composition."

8. It's the middle of my journey, or so it seems. I feel sated with walking, looking, walking on paper. Should I stop and come back later? What do I expect to achieve by continuing to the end besides the satisfaction of finishing the journey I began? What journey am I really on? Where will I be at the end? Am I on some gradient studded with subtle transformations that I at the moment cannot discern? Or is this journey as flat as the smooth brown tile floor on which I walk? The crowd seems to be thinning out (I mistakenly just wrote "want" for "walk"—what do I want?) for lunch. Others have a better sense of boundaries than I do. Some aggressive yet sentimental impulse keeps me blurring the edges of my ordinary good sense of when enough is enough. Do I really have such good sense? I know, however dull and uninterested I may at the moment feel, that I will stay and walk on. For one thing, a lovely etching, done with an electric crayon, of "Mary Cassatt in the Louvre, Museum of Antiques," based on a Japanese silhouette by Katsushika Hokusai, of a flowing woman on a hillside prospect at midday I suspect, looking down at a field and out to the horizon, pleases me too much. Next to the woman in the Japanese print is a bucking horse exploding with sexual energy within inches of her reverie-bound self. Who would not halt before this exhilarating prospect? Mary Cassatt in her Parisian best leans on her umbrella before a painting, and a young girl seated next to her turns from her book and looks with Mary Cassatt. A man in the painting lies on a couch. Perhaps his energy has excited them. Somewhere I walk to this composed, urbane scene with the Japanese bucking horse. In a black-ink monotype next to this a woman langorously puts on her stockings. She seems to be studying her soft body as I am. Aimlessly, irritated, aroused I wander around the room and see in warm burnt-red and black oils a woman bent over her iron, next to which a Daumier laundress walks heavily up some steps, laundry under one arm and a child, fat and ugly, his hand in hers, laboring up some steps. Where is Hephaestos in him? Psyche in her? I can hardly breathe.

9. In the next gallery immediately a woman sitting naked on a bed, breasts out, hand supporting herself on her hips, is having her hair combed by someone whose face disappears off the top of the painting. I have not even journeyed around the room. No time to think or dream. The girls' long hair washes across the front of her maid's white skirt.

They love and hate each other and are aroused. The room is full of pastel nudes. As people walk into this gallery they are being charged with erotic motion. Men seem to loosen up at the joints, the women appear rounder and softer. There are many small bronze sculptures of women drying their bodies. But the towels are textured and muscular, alive, and I can't but think of them as cloudy swans encroaching on half-suspecting Ledas.

10. In the next room I see small bronze horses, powerful, but they don't touch me. They are just miniatures, trotting, leaping, walking. I feel like walking.

11. I'm becoming more aware of my fellow travelers. Like me they seem to be becoming more alive. Everyone is round and animated, drawn into the flesh and motion of "Late Dancers and Singers 1877–1900." All the dancers, each encased in glass, are bronze motion, arm and leg outstretched, flying again and again. Muscular buttocks and legs, leg lifted and bent, held at the foot, with the head twisted down and back to look and judge the position and effect, itself part of the effect. Flesh doesn't hide or diminish the grace, a weighty grace. I have forgotten that I'm walking. A white woman in red stands taut before a dancer, her black lover draws her away from the bronze dancer to himself. Together at a distance they look back at the flying Psyche and slowly circle around her. I slowly get up from my bench in the corner of the room, reluctantly move on. Leaving this gallery is sorrow.

12. In the next room two pastels show peasant dancers, heavy in their peasant clothes, still full of Degas's grace. There are cases of bronze dancers. Circling around one case, I see Spanish dancers with arched backs, in another are dancers on one foot struggling gracefully with stockings, in a third are dancers walking forward with hands on hips. The museum has placed a Delacroix oil of "Christ on the Lake of Gennesaret" in a boat crowned with dark figures (next to Degas's pastel, "Dancer, Pink and Green, about 1890") also in motion, fixing their garments. Finally at the end of the gallery, an inspiration unbidden, perhaps, a bronze nude woman glances back, a "Woman taken Unawares,"

and next to her is a bronze pregnant woman. Her hands are grasped around her big belly behind which are dancers' legs in repose.

13. The last gallery. Tiny photographs by Degas. He is in most of them, here is Mallarmé, there Renoir. Degas grew a beard during all those dancers and horses. Here are Mallarmé and his daughter posed before a painting. In another Degas stands with his niece Odette, in 1900, out on a balcony. He seems framed with her against a rectangle of blackness.

13.

The Bridge

A bridge seems to become an animated path; we feel life and movement in the bridge itself. The words that architects use to characterize bridges imply great potential movement: thrust, strut, suspension, tension, compression. A bridge is not inert.

A "Landscape" by Jacob van Ruisdael displaces the energy and movement of a bridge away from itself. Placed in the center of the painting, the bridge stands empty. It connects a path—beginning in the back or upper right-hand corner and extending into the lower left foreground—on which a man, practically as dark as the dark trees and ground, is plodding slowly toward the bridge from the rear. On the path in the lower left a nobleman on a horse and his "man" standing on the ground holding another horse together form a group that interrupts the sinuous movement of the path and of the stream (which flows more or less straight from front to back). A hunter (the second horseman) and his dog (both nearly invisible from a distance) approach the bridge having startled a fisherman, interrupted him from his eternal leisure on the bank of the river just below the bridge. Everything in the painting centers on the empty, perfect form of the bridge itself, the image of graceful and permanent suspension, modified and jeopardized, however, by the hunter's stealth and imminent revelation and by the fisherman's gaze recently and suddenly averted from its placidity. The bridge here has a kindly function, knitting together the presently disparate human community, providing a register of permanent human relations even though, or perhaps because, the dramatic elements are occurring not on it but only within an area of its influence.

In Constable's "A Bridge, Borrowdale" motion is juxtaposed with timelessness and this juxtaposition conveyed by a female presence "bearing" her load amidst solitary mountains, herself being borne by the low but graceful arch of the bridge that fills most of the painting. Beneath it a river glides at its own sweet will. Its flow is barely perceptible—one almost has to imagine it. The woman reminds me of Wordsworth's famous "spot of time":

> A girl who bore a pitcher on her head
> And seemed with difficult steps to force her way
> Against the blowing wind.[†]

In "View in Borrowdale" Constable has painted the (presumably) same bridge now as the center of a much larger mountainous and watery landscape. At the lower right a man rides out of the picture on an oxcart. Unlike the van Ruisdael there is almost no human presence, and yet the bridge, the human construction, organizes the landscape in the manner of the picturesque. Strangely, in both paintings the arch bridge and its perfect and full reflection in the quiet water beneath it form an eye. And one can imagine it looking out on the quiet scene and giving it shape just as the artist or the viewer looks at and through it for his own ordering. The bridge glimmers in the visionary mode.

What constitutes "vision" in the Constables is the perfection of arched shape organizing large bowls and flats and distances of landscape. The woman walking over the bridge suggests earth-mother archetypes and the melancholy paradoxes of fertility and death. Contrast this bridge with two examples from Claude Monet's Japanese Footbridge series. The feelings of melancholy, intimations of death, are totally irrelevant to these paintings partly because of Monet's relegation of the bridge to an almost completely formal status. In both examples, but particularly the second, our experience of the bridge is less and less that of an instrument of transformation and less and less a principle of human organization in a natural landscape. We know this first of all because Monet created his entire Giverny garden, of which the bridge is part, for the sole purpose of painting it. In all the footbridge paintings we never see the bridge complete, we never see the paths that lead to and from it, only the middle, the span and slight arch of the bridge. Unlike the great stone bridge painted by Constable, itself coming out of the mountainous ground, a bridge that dominates the landscape around it, the Japanese bridge seems light and airy, we see through its structure for the sake of the flowers, water-lilies, bushes, and hanging willows that suffuse the painting. The bridge creates optical oscillations between three and two dimensions; do we look through or at the bridge? Monet demands that we see through the bridge while we look at it, that we see its form providing the primary horizontal movement across the canvas while its color reflects the colors of water, flowers, and greenery around it. Later on in the life of the bridge Monet made trellises for wisteria vines on the bridge, so that, as it took on more and more the texture and meaning of its surroundings, its visual distinction grew increasingly formal. Depth and the full and distinct shape of Constable's bridge, what largely causes the melancholy of the vision, completely gives way in the late Monet to planar surface, the dilution, the near eradication of depth and fine outline. Motion, implied in Constable in the gentle glide of water beneath the certain solidity of granite, here turns not only to the inner life of all solid things but becomes the endless dartings of color that indicate the endless firings of nerves in the eye itself. Even the bridge is a mass of the excitations of the life of the eye. There is no room for thought, imaginings of walkers, paths, before and after, "humanity." All sense of a bridge as the occasion for a pause, the redirection of thought and perception, is absent.

Wordsworth's "Composed Upon Westminster Bridge, September 3, 1802," recalls us to this latter literary response to a bridge. The bridge is the setting for, not the subject of, the poem. It is his perspective: first outward to the mass and myriad of buildings, then inward and backward through implied memory to the analogy with nature, and finally downward (and inward)—"Ne'er saw I, never felt, a calm so deep"—into the depths of himself and the depths of the water beneath him. It is clear from line two that the moment is transitional. One could, were he dull enough, simply pass by, deny the scene its majesty and the bridge its spiritual function. The sonnet, in its short way a perfect vehicle for a brief moment of wondering gaze and meditation, receives the halted traveler's (albeit, in this case, a traveler in a carriage) turn to poetry: simile, analogy, pun, metaphor. Language complicates as the sun steeps and the walker pauses. The deep calm leads to an intuition, perhaps an apprehension, of seeming and, mildly, of deception of the city's own pause before the ominous urban day begins. The poet, we imagine, moves on while the city still allows him his seemings and similes. The poem grows to ripeness under the knowledge that this moment, as well as this walker and therefore this perception, will shortly pass. Its energy and strength lie in the knowledge of its parenthetical existence.[†]

The power of the "mighty heart" of the river under his feet, at this point latent and bringing within itself its intentions for good or for ill, Wordsworth bursts forth in another, later, bridge poem, "To the Torrent at the Devil's Bridge, North Wales, 1824":

> How art thou named? In search of what strange land,
> From what huge height, descending? Can such force
> Of waters issue from a British source,
> Or hath not Pindus fed thee, where the band
> Of Patriots scoop their freedom out, with hand
> Desperate as thine? Or come the incessant shocks
> From that young Stream, that smites the throbbing rocks,
> Of Viamala? There I seem to stand,
> As in life's morn; permitted to behold,
> From the dread chasm, woods climbing above woods,
> In pomp that fades not; everlasting snows;
> And skies that ne'er relinquish their repose;
> Such power possess the family of floods
> Over the minds of Poets, young or old![†]

The bridge has its worldly function: to aid in the communication between people and in the performance of tasks. At the end of Coleridge's "The Nightingale," the worldly function of the bridge—transportation—asserts itself, and the poet reluctantly resumes a journey homeward to family responsibilities:

> Farewell, O Warbler! till to-morrow eve,
> And you, my friends! farewell, a short farewell!

> We have been loitering [on a bridge] long and pleasantly,
> And now for our dear homes.—That strain again!
> Full fain it would delay me![†]

There are many "farewells" here; the bridge pulls strongly. Here is the "illicit" relationship with his friends, the Wordsworths, illicit because it draws Coleridge away from his jealous and estranged wife. But this loitering has other dangers to him that themselves refer inward and then outward to beauty and poetry. They also involve values and choices and questions of freedom. Can one free nature of its traditional associations, can one discover a restorative, communal energy in a nature that has previously been accorded *penseroso* status? Can one live in a world free from myths prescribed by custom? Can one be free of one's own private nightmares? The poem bridges all these questions while the poet and his friends loiter, at twilight, on a bridge:

> No cloud, no relique of the sunken day
> Distinguishes the West, no long thin slip
> Of sullen light, no obscure trembling hues.
> Come, we will rest on this old mossy bridge!
> You see the glimmer of the stream beneath,
> But hear no murmuring: it flows silently,
> O'er its soft bed of verdure. All is still,
> A balmy night! and though the stars be dim,
> Yet let us think upon the vernal showers
> That gladden the green earth, and we shall find
> A pleasure in the dimness of the stars.[†]

Neither a city nor a devil's bridge, this one belongs to moss, captured by nature itself. Almost a thing of nature, its waters afford nothing to the ear and only light to the eye. The opening of the poem, for all of the absences indicated in these lines, is thought full. The poet from the first word thinks about what is absent, indeed creates another scene that nearly supplants the real and present one. Several of Coleridge's monologues begin with the recognition of silence and peace as a signal for the mind to engage its own reality, to imagine, to remember, and then imagine. Thought and physical life interact complementarily; one will "fill up the interspersed vacancies / And momentary pauses" of the other. In this sense "The Eolian Harp," "This Lime-Tree Bower," "Frost at Midnight," and "Dejection" are 'bridge" poems like "The Nightingale." Yet more than these other poems "The Nightingale" puts forward a precariousness in the thoughts of the poet, a daringly elaborated thesis ("In Nature there is nothing melancholy") with continued hints of a subversive resistance to what is essentially a formulation of the possibilities of a fully lived and unselfconscious existence. The resistance takes the form of a fear of loneliness and death and a fear of "death in life": nightmares. Poised on the bridge and over the silent but glimmering stream, the poet walks through his thoughts in a long farewell that he hopes will never end and in which he would like to "bridge" the inevitable departure from his friends with tales of unbroken, intuitive connections between nature and individuals. The tales he re-collects appear as "seemings," since their capacities to bridge or withstand the separation remain untested. The bridge itself, stone yet covered with moss, solid and supportive of both natural and human life, is the opposite of the bridge of words, which is a precarious, uncertain support, having merely filled up an interspersed vacancy of a walk. The hope is that its strength and resilience will reside in its beauty and in its sincerity, that through its peculiarly human vulnerability it will effect a "passage" from one person to another.

The walk serves as setting for such a range of human experience that it would not surprise me to discover a piece of writing that imputed a consciousness to the path or road of the walker. Painters, like Corot and Utrillo, have painted the energy and motion of the street. Monet has granted substance to the bridge. Kafka's "Bridge" tells its own story. Spanning a ravine with a trout stream in it, the bridge existed in a preconscious confusion indefinitely until someone chose to walk across it:

> He came, he tapped me with the iron point of his stick, then he lifted my coattails with it and put them in order upon me. He plunged the point of his stick into my bushy hair and let it lie there for a long time, forgetting me no doubt while he wildly gazed around him. But then—I was just following him in thought over mountain and valley—he jumped with both feet on the middle of my body. I shuddered with wild pain, not knowing what was happening. Who was it? A child? A dream? A wayfarer? A suicide? A tempter? A destroyer? And I turned around so as to see him. A bridge to turn around! I had not yet turned quite around when I already began to fall, I fell and in a

moment I was torn and transpierced by the sharp rocks which had always gazed up at me so peacefully from the rushing water.[†]

This is a parable about the walker who brings the "bridge" into consciousness by destroying it. I think of the Chaucerian meaning of "to tread" here, for this walker does not simply use the bridge as instrument or vehicle but provokes the bridge, aggressively and sexually, harshly. Suddenly the bridge is flooded with questions about human beings, questions that seem to erupt from no recognizable point in the bridge's history. It is provoked into two of the archetypal gestures of spiritual consciousness, the fall and the conversion ("I turned around"). At the point of the telling, the bridge has become a person, recalling—or is it creating, constructing?—a dream of prehuman existence, a time before the drives, before the fantasies of desire and death, before the social encounter, the time that Wordsworth describes as wandering lonely as a cloud. The bridge anticipated the walker with thoroughly innocent elation. His arrival means the ugly death of both elation and innocence.

But what of the walker's fate? Did he fall to his death in the roaring stream below? Does the walker and the bridge (that turned on him like an animal) collapse into this storytelling, commemorating, disembodied voice, like Orpheus?

THE WALK: NOTES ON A ROMANTIC IMAGE

Epilogue

I. The Fool (Tarot)

With light step, as if earth and its trammels had little power to restrain him, a young man in gorgeous vestments pauses at the brink of a precipice among the great heights of the world; he surveys the blue distance before him—its expanse of sky rather than the prospect below. His act of eager walking is still indicated, though he is stationary at the given moment; his dog is still bounding. The edge which opens on the depth has no terror; it is as if angels were waiting to uphold him, if it came about that he leaped from the height. His countenance is full of intelligence and expectant dream. . . . He is a prince of the other world on his travels through this one—all amidst the morning glory, in the keen air. The sun, which shines behind him, knows whence he came, whither his is going, and how he will return by another path after many days. He is the spirit in search of experience.[†]

Arthur Edward Waite, *The Pictorial Key to the Tarot*

Wordsworth to Whitman to Robert Walser (*The Walk*) and back as far as Aeneas landing at Carthage, waking up in the morning of the unknown land, to walk out to discover it, all join the vision of the Tarot fool.

"The Fool," Tarot Pack. Courtesy of U.S. Games Systems.

Why fool?—because his innocence of danger and doubt and social encumbrance releases in him energy and joyful vision. The necessities of life lie in his bag, the gold rose of beauty shines in his delicate hand. "Instinct" (like the dog in the Snowdon climb in *The Prelude*) is the playful dog at his side. Only the world considers him foolish: they see him about to fall off the cliff. In eternity they see that his spirit will buoy him up.

In the *I Ching* "treading" was more than an expression of innocent energy and faith: it established a condition of conduct, of social and moral discriminations, and of the relationship between self-knowledge and action. "Heaven above, and the lake below, . . . Thus the superior man discriminates between high and low, / and thereby fortifies the thinking of the people."[†] The world of the person as walker is very alive and responsive; the walker has an effect on himself and on others. Thus "to tread" is to tread on the tail of the tiger. How will it react? One needs to progress in life—to make decisions and move forward out of desire and one's urges—with decorum. ("Pleasant manners succeed even with irritable people.")[†] Decorum applies to oneself as well as to others; it is a vigilance about the effects of one's purpose. The tiger bites when one acts out of restlessness and dissatisfaction and an ambition that contradicts the life of simplicity. The tiger bites when one misjudges oneself, undertaking something beyond one's strength. But caution and circumspection, "perseverance with awareness of danger," lead ultimately to good fortune.[†]

II. The Walk and Silence

Walking recently on Sixth Avenue in Manhattan at midday, I suddenly realized that Baudelaire's and Poe's metaphor for the sound of the mass of urban walkers—the roar—no longer applied. I heard lots of noise, but I could not describe it as a roar, the cry of a lion, the massive, monolithic impenetrable sound of a waterfall, the crashing or beating of waves, the rumble of a tornado. Nature could provide for me no suitable image. To begin with, there was not one phalanx of sound but a great number of various sounds. The results were loud, but—on the one hand—they were largely metallic, mechanical, electrical. They were often rubbing sounds, things (like brakes) being rubbed unnaturally close together or being pounded (the pavement by jackhammers) with unnaturally fast and hard blows. The sounds ranged, it seemed, over several octaves with relentless dissonances. The human sounds were not as invasive as the word "roar" would predict. They did not invite metaphor, being too much themselves—discreet utterances or (as one walked by) parts of utterances—rather comforting actually since the part always assures one that there is a whole, that two people trust in the fullness of their conversation, or that the monologuing walker trusts in the complete unity of his peripatetic psychosis.

The variety of sounds makes one aware of the spaces around them. It makes one aware of silence, of silence in the packed city at midday. And if he chooses to focus on it, one can hear footsteps.

Footsteps remind us of the silence that always encircles the walker while it insists that the silence of the walker can never be complete. Blaise Cendrars says beautifully that at evening the shadows fill up footprints. We can add that silence too fills up footsteps. Walking across an alpine meadow, a tiny marsh buttercup may bend beneath my boot silently, yet the steps are heard against the granite. On the walk the silence surrounds us as presence but also as an intimation of what is not far off.

Near the outset of Walter Benjamin's portrait of Moscow as he observed it walking, we meet the following sentences: "Only he who, by decision, has made his dialectical peace with the world can grasp the concrete. But someone who wishes to decide 'on the basis of facts' will find no basis in the facts."[†] Part of the silence of walking may lie in the plowed ground of these mental preparations. The mind is now fertile for the facts or impressions the walker will encounter. Noise, in the sense of bombardment or assault from the active world through which one passes, may indicate the unprepared mind. The great advantage for the walker is that one can pass through the world as a conscious being—more particularly, and this I think is the "dialectical peace" to which Benjamin refers, as at once a social and politically irritated being (irritated by the effects of capitalism) and a spiritual being sublimely exalted above and mollified by the scenes of societal imposition upon natural and human landscapes: the peace is an acceptance of both self and world, as occasionally and fundamentally as compatible or incompatible as they may seem. Another walker's dialectic emerges in the flicker of aesthetic perspective. Some walkers, like Benjamin, can see (or he might say, decide to see) the world as scenic, as stopping a chance moment that, in the city at least, is also typical and characteristic. But many writers frame what they see in an idyllic distance, in Romantic art. Part of the pleasure of the walk lies in this comfortable exercise, which affirms the walker or an individual celebrating mind and body and the rhythms of life. Generally the walker who writes about walking extends the aesthetics of individuality into language. But there are those, like Benjamin, who insist on dialectical peace, on individuality as at once counter to and instrumental for the sociological observation of the world. They see themselves as at once an anonymous piece of the world and an imposition upon it.

The individual as an abstraction: desire, intention, imposition, participation. The walker becomes the simplicity of ourselves, at once a passerby and a depositor of imprints, traces, marks. The world is at once untouched and touched by the walker's passage. The artist Richard Long has come closer than anyone in our time to representing (in photographs, sculptures, and maps) the abstraction of the walk of the person. He takes a picture of the land over which he has walked and calls it *Line Made by Walking*. He walks in a straight line from here to there, retracing his steps enough times so that the imprint of his walking on the landscape comes clear. He rarely appears in his own pictures: only the "walk" itself, the human imposition on the landscape. Sometimes he places stones at precise intervals on his walk, another kind of imposition, yet hardly the Romantic imposition of "Man's inhumanity to man." The world—in any social or ecological sense—remains the same, only revered a bit more. The reverence itself is a trace, a mark seen, and in noting it (writing it), we ourselves mark the beauty, in its simplicity, of our desire.

Notes

Page 4: [Reading Proust] Roland Barthes, "On Reading," in *The Rustle of Language*, trans. Richard Howard (New York: Hill and Wang, Ferrar, Straus and Giroux, 1986), 41.

Page 4: [In this Perspective] Ibid.

Page 7: [Now it appears] John Keats, "To J. H. Reynolds, 19 February 1818," in *Letters of John Keats*, ed. Robert Gittings (London: Oxford University Press, 1970), 66.

Page 9: [My foot is] Richard M. Griffith, "Anthropodology: Man A-Foot," in *The Philosophy of the Body: Rejections or Cartesian Dualism*, ed. Stuart F. Spicker (Chicago: Quadrangle Books, 1970), 279–80.

Page 9: [has no Longer] Alice Meynell, "The Foot," in *Essays* (London: Burns Oates & Washbourne Ltd., 1925), 100.

Page 10: [to walk Abroad] Thomas Traherne, "Walking," in *Seventeenth-Century Prose and Poetry*, 2d ed., ed. Alexander M. Witherspoon and Frank J. Warnke (New York: Harcourt Brace Jovanovich, 1982), 1029.

Page 10: [the police spoils] William Hazlitt, "On Poetry in General," in *Selected Essays or William Hazlitt: 1778–1830*, ed. Geoffrey Keynes (New York: Random House, 1948; London: The Nonesuch Press, 1930), 398.

Page 10: [This Vegetable World] William Blake, "Milton," in *The Complete Poetry and Prose or William Blake*, newly rev., ed. David V. Erdman (Garden City: Anchor, Doubleday, 1982), book 1, lines 12–14, p. 115.

Page 10: [Walk his legs off] Charles Lamb, "To William Wordsworth: 20th

March, 1822," in *The Portable Charles Lamb: Letters and Essays*, ed. John Mason Brown (New York: Viking Press, 1949), 157.

Page 11: [I have . . . been moulting] John Keats, "To J. H. Reynolds, 11 July 1819, in *Letters of John Keats: A New Selection*, ed. Robert Gittings (London: Oxford University Press, 1970), 268.

Page 11: [Flectere] Sigmund Freud, "The Interpretation of Dreams," in *The Basic Writings of Sigmund Freud*, ed. A. A. Brill (New York: Modern Library, Random House, 1938), 179.

Page 11: [must limp] Charles Lamb, "My relations," in *The Portable Lamb*, 217.

Page 12: [I have two doctors] George Macaulay Trevelyan, *Walking* (Hartford: Edwin Valentine Mitchell, 1928), 19.

Pages 12–13: [Like Stalks] Pablo Neruda, "Ritual of My Legs," in *Pablo Neruda, Five Decades: A Selection (Poems: 1925–1970)*, ed. and trans. Ben Belitt (New York: Grove Press, 1974), 16–21.

Page 13: [fethered Pertelote] Geoffrey Chaucer, "The Nun's Priest's Tale," "The Canterbury Tales," in *The Works of Geoffrey Chaucer*, 2d ed., ed. F. N. Robinson (Boston: Houghton Mifflin; the Riverside Press; F. N. Robinson, 1957), lines 3177–78, p. 203.

Page 13: [when shall we tread] Blake, "Milton," in *Complete Poetry*, line 45, p. 119.

Page 13: [How red the Sons] Ibid., line 4, p. 124.

Page 13: [Had I the heaven's] William B. Yeats, "He wishes for the cloths of Heaven," in *Chief Modern poets of Britain and America, Vol. I: Poets of Britain*, 5th ed., ed. Gerald DeWitt Sanders, John Herbert Nelson, and M. L. Rosenthal (London: Collier-Macmillan, 1970), 1–100.

Page 13: [whilst from off] John Milton, "Comus," in *John Milton: Complete Poems and Major Prose*, ed. Merritt Y. Hughes (New York: Odyssey Press, 1957), lines 896–99, p. 15.

Page 14: [yes I will be] John Keats, "Ode to Psyche," in *John Keats and Percy Bysshe Shelley: Complete Poetical Works* (New York: Modern Library, n.d.), lines 50–51, p. 187.

Page 14: [Generations have trod] Gerard Manley Hopkins, "God's Grandeur," in *The Poems of Gerard Manley Hopkins*, 4th ed., ed. W. H. Gardner and N. H. Mackenzie (London: Oxford University Press, 1967), line 5, p. 66.

Page 14: [No hungry] Keats, "Ode to a Nightingale," *Keats and Shelley*, line 62, p. 184.

Page 17: [For in this walk] Conrad Aiken, "The Walk in the Garden," in *A Letter from Li Po and Other Poems* (New York: Oxford University Press, 1955), 64–65.

Page 17: [Give me the . . . sky] William Hazlitt, "On Going a Journey," in *William Hazlitt: Selected Writings*, ed. Ronald Blythe (Baltimore: Penguin Books, 1970), 137.

Page 18: [I do not approve] Robert Louis Stevenson, "Walking Tours," in *The Lore of the Wanderer: an Open-air Anthology*, ed. George Goodchild (London: J. M. Dent & Sons, n.d.), 9.

Page 18: [that burthen] William Wordsworth, *The Prelude: 1799, 1805, 1850: Authoritative Texts, Context and Reception, Recent Critical Essays*, ed. Jonathan Wordsworth, M. H. Abrams, and Stephen Gill (New York: W. W. Norton, 1970), book 1, lines 23–25 (1805), pp. 28–30.

Page 19: [oh Welcome messenger] Ibid., lines 5–19.

Pages 19–20: [afoot and light-hearted] Walt Whitman, "Song of the Open Road," in *Leaves of Grass and Selected Prose*, ed. Sculley Bradley (New York: Holt, Rinehart and Winston, 1960), lines 1–15, p. 124.

Page 20: [the World] Milton, "Paradise Lost," in *Complete Poems*, book 12, lines 646–49, p. 469.

Page 21: [when it looks] Franz Kafka, "A Sudden Walk," in *The Complete Stories*, ed. Nahum N. Glatzen (New York: Schocken Books, 1983), 397–98.

Page 22: [Grasmere looked] Dorothy Wordsworth, "The Grasmere Journals, 1800–1803," in *Journals of Dorothy Wordsworth*, vol. 1, ed. E. de Selincourt (London: Macmillan, 1941), p. 50.

Page 22: [breathless grey] Ibid., II:184.

Page 23: [a traveller] William Wordsworth, *Resolution and Independence in Wordsworth: Poetical Works*, ed. Thomas Hutchinson, new ed. rev. by Ernest de Selincourt (London: Oxford University Press, 1981), 155–57 passim.

Page 23: [those walks] William Wordsworth, *The Prelude: 1799, 1805, 1850*, book 4, lines 126–48 (1805), p. 132.

Pages 24–25: ["what, you are] Wordsworth, "Stepping Westward," in *Poetical Works*, 229.

Pages 26–27: [a shadow that grows] Denise Levertov, "Stepping Westward," in *The Sorrow Dance* (New York: New Directions, 1966), 15–16.

Page 27: [I wandered lonely] W. Wordsworth, "I Wandered Lonely as a Cloud," *Poetical Works*, 149.

Page 27: [when this man] Paul Valery, *The Art of Poetry*, trans. Denise Folliot (New York: Vintage Books, 1961), 208.

Page 28: [goes nowhere] Ibid., 207.

Page 29: [lap us about] Virginia Woolf, "The Modern Essay," in *The Common Reader* (New York: Harcourt Brace and World, 1923), 217.

Page 31: [should lay us] Ibid., 217.

Page 31: [as a punishment] E. V. Lucas, "Journey Round a Room," in *Turning*

Things Over (New York: E. P. Dutton and Company, 1929), 59–60.

Pages 32–33: [among the silver] Ibid., 65–66.

Page 33: [Writers . . . are really] Walter Benjamin, "Unpacking my Library," in *Illuminations*, ed. Hannah Arendt (New York: Harcourt Brace and World, 1968), 61.

Page 34: [To come to Keats] A. A. Milne, "My Library," in *Not That It Matters* (New York: E. P. Dutton and Company, 1920), 13.

Page 34: [thus there is] Benjamin, "Unpacking," 60.

Page 36: [walks. The body] Jules Renard, "December, 1907," in *The Journal of Jules Renard*, ed. and trans. Louise Bogan and Elizabeth Roset (New York: George Braziller, 1964), 221.

Page 36: [Louis Aragon] Louis Aragon, *Nightwalker* (*Le Paysan de Paris*), trans. Frederick Brown (Englewood Cliffs: Prentice-Hall, 1970), 5.

Page 36: [. . . this cave] James Wright, "The Jewel," in *The Branch Will Not Break* (Middletown: Wesleyan University Press, 1963), 17.

Page 36: [As a man] Homer, *The Iliad of Homer*, trans. Richard Lattimore (Chicago: Phoenix Press, University of Chicago Press, 1951), book 3, lines 33–37, p. 101.

Page 42: ["Quite Early] Dylan Thomas, "Quite Early One Morning," in *Quite Early One Morning* (New York: New Directions, 1954), 12–19 passim.

Page 44: [My old Friend] Hazlitt, "Going on a Journey," 139.

Page 45: [with change of place] Ibid., 144.

Page 45: [We measure] Ibid., 145.

Page 46: [Watt's way] Samuel Beckett, *Watt* (New York: Grove Press, 1959), 30.

Page 47: [From an erroneous] James Boswell, *Boswell's Journal of a Tour to the Hebrides with Samuel Johnson, LL.D.: 1773*, new ed., ed. Frederick A. Pottle and Charles H. Bennett (New York: Yale University, McGraw-Hill Book Co., 1961), 33.

Page 47: [Dinner was mentioned] Ibid., 42.

Page 47: [This is roving] Ibid., 328.

Page 47: [what an addition] Ibid., 331.

Page 48: [what a large volume] Laurence Sterne, *A Sentimental Journey* (New York: New American Library, 1964), 36.

Page 48: [I declare, said I,] Ibid., 36–37.

Page 49: [Grasmere looked] D. Wordsworth, "Grasmere Journals," 50.

Page 49: [thus I was going] Ibid., 125.

Page 49: [As we came] Ibid., 126.

Page 49: [In a while the pitch] Marye Piercy, "Sand Roads," in *Living in the Open* (New York: Alfred A. Knopf, 1982), 1. "Sand Roads," 22.

Page 49: [Follow the ax cut] Ibid., 4. "Paradise Hollow," 23–24.

Page 49: [In wilderness I] Gretel Ehrlich, "Introduction: Sierra Club Wilderness Calendar" (Shell: Gretel Ehrlich, n.d.), 1.

Page 50: [Walking is also] Ibid.

Page 50: [to find wildness] Ibid., 2.

Page 50: [there are dunes] A. R. Ammons, *Collected Poems: 1951–1971* (New York: W. W. Norton & Co., 1927), 148.

Page 50: [you are standing] Piercy, "Sand Roads," 8. "The road behind the last dune," 29.

Pages 50–51: [lies down before] Ibid., 30.

Page 51: [Afterwards William] D. Wordsworth, "Grasmere Journal" (1802), 139.

Page 52: ['Tis restless magic] William Wordsworth, *An Evening Walk*, ed. James Averill, *The Cornell Wordsworth*, gen. ed. Stephen Parish (Ithaca: Cornell University Press, 1984) (1793), line 345, p. 70.

Page 52: [Sweetly ferocious] Ibid., 46.

Page 52: [He swells his] Ibid., lines 201–206, p. 56.

Page 53: [thy trees take root] George Gordon Lord Byron, "Childe Harold's Pilgrimage," in *Selected Poetry of Lord Byron*, rev. ed., ed. Leslie A. Marchaud (New York: Modern Library, Random House, 1967), canto 3, verse 99, line 3, p. 104.

Page 53: [I walk as ere] Alfred Lord Tennyson, "In Memoriam A. H. H.," in *Poems of Alfred Lord Tennyson*, ed. Charles Tennyson (London: Collins, 1954), verse 68, lines 5–8, p. 327.

Page 53: [We pass] Ibid., verse 73, lines 9–10, p. 330.

Page 53: [Hardy: Return] Thomas Hardy, *The Return of the Native*, ed. George Woodcock (New York: Penguin Books, 1978), 53–57 passim.

Page 57: [Yet it is that] Thomas Hardy, "The Dead Man Walking," in *The Variorum Edition of The Complete poems of Thomas Hardy*, ed. James Gibson (Macmillan Publishing Co., 1978), 219.

Page 59: [In this little book] Bashō, *The Narrow Road to the Deep North and Other Travel Sketches*, trans. Nobuyuki Yuasa (New York: Penguin Books, 1966), postscript, 143.

Page 59: [As firmly] Ibid., 142.

Page 60: [It looks as if] Ibid., 112.

Page 60: [Rid of my hair] Ibid., 100–101.

Page 60: [Amid mountains] Ibid., 103.

Page 60: [A thicket] Ibid., 118.

Page 61: [I am awe-struck] Ibid., 134.

Page 61: [no matter where] Ibid., 136.

Page 61:   [Soon, oh how Soon]   Hermann Hesse, *Wandering: Notes and Sketches by Hermann Hesse*, trans. James Wright (New York: Farrar, Straus & Giroux, 1972), 83.

Page 63:   [At length, as we]   Henry David Thoreau, "A Walk to Wachusett," in *Thoreau: The Major Essays*, ed. Jeffrey L. Duncan (New York: E. P. Dutton & Co., 1972), 37.

Pages 63–64:   [Men walk]   Ralph Waldo Emerson, "Circles," in *Essays: First Series* (Boston: Houghton, Mifflin & Co., 1883), p. 285.

Page 64:   [In nature every moment]   Ralph Waldo Emerson, "Circles," 298.

Page 64:   [The one thing]   Ibid., 300.

Page 64:   [We go eastward]   Thoreau, "Walking," in *Major Essays*, 204.

Page 65:   [The eye is the first]   Emerson, "Circles," 281.

Page 65:   [you may go round]   Thoreau, "Walking," 202.

Page 65:   [On every side]   Thoreau, "Wachusett," 35.

Page 66:   [Literature . . . is]   Emerson, "Circles," 291.

Page 66:   [Opening the gate]   Thoreau, "A Winter Walk," in *Major Essays*, 41.

Page 66:   [Meanwhile we step]   Ibid., 43.

Pages 66–67:   [No domain]   Ibid., 52.

Page 67:   [all elements]   Ibid., 40–56 passim.

Pages 67–68:   [where are the Songs]   Keats, "To Autumn," in *Poetical Works*, 193–94 passim.

Page 68:   [no arranged terror]   Ammons, "Corsons Inlet," 151.

Page 68:   [I went for a walk]   Ibid., 147–48.

Page 68:   [ever-hooded . . . Sea]   Wallace Stevens, "The Idea of Order at Key West," in *The Palm at the End of the Mind: Selected Poems and a Play by Wallace Stevens*, ed. Holly Stevens (New York: Vintage Books, Random House, 1972), 97–99 passim.

Page 69:   [Perpendicular . . . thought]   Ammons, "Corsons Inlet," 148.

Page 69:   [Scope Eludes]   Ibid., 151.

Page 69:   [risk is full]   Ibid., 149.

Pages 70–71:   [Never did I think]   Jean-Jacques Rousseau, *The Confessions of Jean-Jacques Rousseau*, trans. J. M. Cohen (Baltimore: Penguin Books, 1954), 157–58.

Page 72:   [To travel on Foot]   Jean-Jacques Rousseau, *Emile or On Education*, trans. Allan Bloom (New York: Basic Books, 1979), 412.

Pages 72–73:   [sat . . . on a cushion]   Jean-Jacques Rousseau, *Reveries of the Solitary Walker*, trans. Peter France (New York: Penguin Books, 1979), "Seventh Walk," 118.

Page 74:   [I walked down]   John Clare, "Journey Out of Essex," in *John Clare,* ed. Eric Robinson and David Powell, *The Oxford Authors*, gen. ed. Frank Kermode (Oxford: Oxford University Press, 1984), 432.

Page 74: [the road on the left] Ibid., 433.

Page 75: [I then suddenly] Ibid., 434.

Page 75: [I then got up] Ibid., 436.

Page 75: [one solitary Overriding] Werner Herzog, *Of Walking in Ice: Munich-Paris, 11/23–12/14, 1974*, trans. Martje Herzog and Alan Greenberg (New York: Tanam Press, 1980), 7–8.

Page 76: [the cigarette packages] Ibid., 24.

Page 76: [why is walking] Ibid., 27.

Page 76: [I was embarrassed] Ibid., 90.

Page 77: [the free soul] Ann Finch, Countess of Winchelsea, "A Nocturnal Reverie," in *The Women Poets in English: An Anthology*, ed. Ann Stanford (New York: Herder and Herder, McGraw-Hill Book Co., 1972), 77–78 passim.

Page 77: [divinist Melancholy] Milton, "Il Penseroso," in *Complete Poems*, lines 12–16, p. 72.

Page 78: [Respice nunc] D. Iuvii Iuvenalis, "Satira 3," in *Satirae with A Literal English Prose Translation and Notes*, vol. 1, ed. John Delaware Lewis (New York: Macmillan and Co., 1882), 37.

Page 78: [Let Constant vigilance] John Gay, "Trivia; or, the Art of Walking the Streets of London," in *The Poetical Works of John Gay*, ed. G. C. Faber (London: Oxford University Press, 1926), book 3, "Of Walking Streets by Night," p. 81.

Page 78: [oh, may thy] Ibid., 84.

Page 78: [Consider, reader] Ibid., 87.

Page 79: [the clock has] Oliver Goldsmith, "Letter CVXII: A City Nightpiece," in *The Citizen of the World*, "Collected Works of Oliver Goldsmith," vol. 2, ed. Arthur Friedman (Oxford: Clarendon Press, 1966), 452.

Page 79: [What cities] Ibid., 452–53.

Page 80: [sleep is equally] Samuel Johnson, "Sleep," in *The Idler* and *The Adventurer*, ed. W. J. Bate, John M. Bullitt, and L. F. Powell (New Haven: Yale University Press, 1963), 99.

Page 80: [strangers, wanderers] Goldsmith, "A City Nightpiece," 453.

Page 80: [Why, why was I born] Ibid., 454.

Page 81: [When a church clock] Charles Dickens, "Nightwalks," in *Lore of the Wanderer*, 71–72.

Page 81: [My principle object] Ibid., 63.

Page 82: [under a kind] Ibid., 65.

Page 82: [And it is not] Ibid., 75.

Page 82: [No time abates] James Thomson, "The City or Dreadful Night," in *Poems and Some Letters of James Thomson*, ed. Anne Rider (Southern Illinois University Press; Centaur Press, 1963), section 3, lines 22–28, p. 182.

Page 83: [Inanimate objects] Leigh Hunt, "Walks Home by Night," in *Essays by Leigh Hunt*, ed. Arthur Symons (London: Walter Scott Publishing Co., n.d.), 47.

Page 83: [I see him now] Ibid., 48.

Page 83: [Never-to-be-forgotten] Ibid.

Page 83: [the town was not] Dylan Thomas, "Quite Early One Morning," in *Quite Early One Morning* (New York: New Directions, 1954), 14.

Page 84: [thus some of the Voices] Ibid., 19.

Page 84: [But here we must] Virginia Woolf, "Street Haunting," in *The Death of the Moth and Other Essays* (New York: Harvest Book, Harcourt Brace Jovanovich, 1970), 23.

Page 84: [when suddenly] Ibid., 26.

Pages 84–85: [the shell-like covering] Ibid., 22.

Page 85: [set about her masterpiece] Ibid., 28–29.

Page 85: [Find anchorage] Ibid., 29–36 passim.

Pages 85–86: [Into each] Ibid., 35.

Page 86: [recalls better places] Leslie Stephen, "In Praise of Walking," in *Studies of a Biographer* (Second Series), vol. 3 (London, 1902), 284.

Page 86: [the devil was still] Leslie Stephen, "London Walks," *Cornhill Magazine*, XLI (1880), 224.

Page 87: [succeed in piercing] Ibid., 234.

Page 89: [two notes, tonic] Thomas Mann, "A Man and His Dog," in *Thomas Mann: Stories of Three Decades*, trans. H. T. Lowe-Porter (New York: Alfred A. Knopf, 1941), 438.

Page 90: [they have not been] Ibid., 466–67.

Page 91: [A city sidewalk] Jane Jacobs, *The Death and Life of Great American Cities* (New York: Vintage Books, Random House, 1961), 30.

Page 91: [A city cannot be] Ibid., 372.

Page 91: [the heart-of-the-city] Ibid., 51.

Pages 91–92: [Under the seeming] Ibid., 50.

Pages 94–97: [In his loneliness] Samuel Taylor Coleridge, "The Rime of the Ancient Mariner," in *The Norton Anthology of English Literature, rev. ed., vol.* 2, ed. M. H. Abrams, E. Talbot Donaldson, Hallett Smith, Robert M. Adams, Samuel Holt Monk, George H. Ford, and David Daiches (New York: W. W. Norton & Co., 1968), Part 4, 222.

Page 97: [the Pleasure of being] Charles Baudelaire, *Intimate Journals*, trans.

Christopher Isherwood (San Francisco: City Lights Books, 1983), 21.

Page 97: [Sexuality is the] Ibid., 87.

Page 97: [this divine prostitution] Charles Baudelaire, "The Crowd," in *Paris Spleen: 1869*, trans. Louis Varèse (New York: New Directions, 1970), 20.

Page 97: [what oddities] Baudelaire, "Miss Bistoury," Ibid., 98.

Pages 97–98: [Just now as I] Charles Baudelaire, "Loss of a Halo," in *Paris Spleen: 1869*, 94.

Page 98: [enjoying a crowd] Ibid., "Intimate Journals," 21.

Page 99: [the substitution of] Gustave LeBon, "Arthur's Pieface," in *The Crowd: A Study of the Popular Mind* (London: Ernest Benn Limited, 1952), 6.

Page 99: [is it not the genius] Ibid., 10.

Page 99: [why should I drive] Baudelaire, *Paris Spleen*, 49.

Page 100: [The truth is] Thomas De Quincey, *Confessions of an Opium Eater*, ed. Alethea Hayter (New York: Penguin Books, 1971), 49–50.

Page 101: [Pursued through many] De Quincey, "Appendix B: Selected Passages from the 1856 Revision," 139.

Page 101: [The true object] Thomas De Quincey, "Susperia De Profundis: Being a Sequel to the Confessions of an English Opium Eater," in *Prose of the British Romantic Movement*, ed. John R. Nabholtz (New York: Macmillan Publishing Co., 1974), 601.

Pages 102–103: [Far from experiencing] Walter Benjamin, "On Some Motifs in Baudelaire," in *Illuminizations: Essays and Reflections*, ed. and intro. Hannah Arendt, trans. Harry Zohn (New York: Harcourt Brace & World, 1955), 171.

Page 103: [Mark in every Face] Blake, "London," in *Complete Poetry*, 26.

Page 104: [On Brooklyn Bridge] Charles Reznikoff, "Rhythms: 1918," in *Poems 1918–1936, vol. 1 of the Complete Poems of Charles Reznikoff*, ed. Seamus Cooney (Santa Barbara: Black Sparrow, 1976), section 7, p. 14.

Page 113: [A girl, who bore] W. Wordsworth, "The Prelude" (1805), book II, lines 305–307, p. 432.

Pages 114–15: [composed upon Westminster Bridge] W. Wordsworth, "Composed Upon Westminster Bridge, September, 1802," in *Poetical Works*, 214.

Page 115: [How art thou] W. Wordsworth, "To the Torrent at the Devil's Bridge, North Wales, 1824," in *Poetical Works*, 216.

Pages 115–16: [Farewell, O Warbler] Samuel Taylor Coleridge, "The Nightingale, a Conversation Poem, April, 1798," in *Major British Poets of the Romantic Period*, ed. William Heath (New York: Macmillan Publishing Co., 1973), lines 87–91, p. 469–70.

Page 116: [No Cloud, no relique] Ibid., lines 1–11.

Pages 117–18: [He came, he tapped] Kafka, "The Bridge," in *Complete Stories*, 411–12.

Page 119: [with light step] Arthur Edward Waite, *The Pictorial Key to the Tarot: (Being Fragments of a Secret Tradition Under the Veil of Divination)* (San Francisco: Harper & Row, 1971), 152–55.

Page 121: [Heaven above] Richard Wilhelm, trans. "Lü/Treading [conduct]," in *The I Ching*, rendered in English by Cary F. Baynes, Foreword by C. G. Jung (New York: Princeton University Press, 1977; Bollingen Foundation, 1967), 45.

Page 121: [Pleasant manners] Ibid., 44.

Page 121: [Perseverance with awareness] Ibid., 47.

Page 122: [Only he who] Walter Benjamin, *Reflections: Essays, Aphorisms, Autobiographical Writings*, ed. Peter Demetz (New York: Harcourt Brace Jovanovich, 1978), 97–98.

Bibliographical Essay

I run into a to me previously unknown piece of walking literature about once every two weeks, a first-rate example about once every two or three months. No longer does this astonish me. After all, walking is the basic way of getting around, even now, with the compulsive dependence on the automobile. So it is a basic vantage point of seeing, and perceiving, the world. Many walking pieces naturally do not draw attention to walking but simply assume the condition of walking the way a singer assumes the air he/she breathes. But for most writers walking occasions or is produced by some perception about "the modern world": nostalgia for a "simpler" time, recovery of "self" in a self-inimical age, an ecological consciousness and a love of the intimate stories nature tells, a perception of the city as self-inimical, the opposite perception that one can mark the amazing variety of persons and language in the city and through this variety note "all at once" the inequities of class and race. Every literary genre welcomes the walk. I propose, therefore, in this brief bibliographical essay merely to indicate by way of supplement to the rest of my book some directions for further reading in a very large literature.

I have no better place to begin than with a beautiful pastoral walking dialogue, which opens: "Whenever we get the feeling the world is going to hell in a handbasket, my friend Jeff Robinson and I go for a walk together." This is a walking essay by Tom Wolf, "A New Walk Is a New Walk" (*The Walking Magazine*, Fall 1986, 62–68). Here an ecological concern organizes the experience and pleasure in nature. In many walking pieces ecology remains latent or absent, but nature focuses a major category of walking literature. Romantic poets, such as Wordsworth and Clare, and essayists, like Leigh Hunt, William Hazlitt, and Thomas De Quincey (*Confessions of an English Opium Eater*), of course, establish nature-walking literature. But it appears throughout the popular magazines of the nineteenth century, in Britain and in the American Thoreau in *Walden* and the Journals (as well as in the essays discussed in this book), and in the poems of Whitman.

More recently nature-walk literature has become very popular in North America, often in the tradition of Thoreau. I mention only two currently popular books of prose: Annie Dillard's *Pilgrim at Tinker Creek* (New York: Bantam, 1975) and Edward Hoagland's *Walking the Dead Diamond River* (San Francisco: North Point Press, 1985). Dillard records one of the nature walker's favorite moments, the new morning:

> The morning woods were utterly new. A strong yellow light pooled between the trees; my shadow appeared and vanished on the path, since a third of the trees I walked under were still bare, a third spread a luminous haze wherever they grew, and another third blocked the sun with new, whole leaves. The snakes were out—I saw a bright, smashed one on the path—and the butterflies were vaulting and furling about; the phlox was at its peak, and even the evergreens looked greener, newly created and washed. (p. 110)

(For a British version of *Pilgrim*, read Flora Thompson's *A Country Calendar*—New York: Oxford, 1984.)

The poet Gary Snyder has reshaped the American nature-walking tradition (primarily in a western-American landscape) through imitation of Chinese and Japanese walking idioms in *The Back Country* (New York: New Directions, 1968). And one must not forget the ancient Chinese poets themselves who wrote walking poems, if one can so speak, of the greatest authenticity. There are lines from Meng Chiao that, though not about walking, comprise a typical (to a Westerner) vision of the Chinese walker:

> When the twisted tree at last shall be my body
> Then I shall begin to live out my natural span.

As he predicts his body's oneness with natural objects, its rootedness in things, he also envisions and shapes his futurity. He produces in me that cleansing sensation that "forever" belongs to the moment, the moment is far away and therefore forever the object of our yearning. The road, or mountain path, in Chinese poetry occasions that same sense of groundedness or security and longing. See *Poems of the Late T'ang*, trans. A. C. Graham (Baltimore: Penguin Books, 1965) and

Lu Yu, *The Wild Old Man*, trans. David M. Gordon (San Francisco: North Point Press, 1984).

Walking literature can turn imperceptibly into travel literature, which by and large does not interest me. In travel literature the act of walking and the pleasure in it tends (there are exceptions) to vanish before interest in what is being encountered. But three books that manage to bridge the categories need mention: Eric Newby, *A Traveller's Life* (London: Picador, 1983); Laurie Lee, *As I Walked Out One Midsummer Morning* (New York: W. W. Norton, 1985), in a sumptuously illustrated edition; and Aldous Huxley, *Along the Road: Notes and Essays of a Tourist* (London: Paladin, 1985). This last, a jewel of a book, combines the perfect balance of the idyllic vision of walking and traveling pleasure, the attention to exquisite detail of observation and of refined pleasure in observation, and the easy flow from objects of nature into objects of high culture. What is more, Huxley's essays are short, which, in this kind of writing, concentrates the pleasure they give: essays on "Books for the Journey," "The Palio at Siena," "Breughel," "Work and Leisure," "Views of Holland."

In the late nineteenth century people began to associate walking with health and pleasure. The two themes stride down the decades to the present. I will mention my favorite recent "how-to" walking book: *The Magic of Walking*, by Aaron Sussman and Ruth Goode (New York: Simon and Schuster, 1967). Not only does it try to generate the reader (in great detail) of the healthful and pleasurable rewards of walking and in congenial prose, but it also has one of the best available anthologies (and a bibliography) of prose about walking.

This is the moment to mention that the current anthologies have a serious limitation: they recreate an impression that all walking ruralizes the imagination and that walking is primarily a "gentle" art, or sport. (Even a stridently critical and left-wing walker like Hazlitt gets absorbed through the anthologies into the atmosphere and assumptions of gentlemen—and I do mean gentle*men*.) But not all walking, and walking literature, yields the imagination the pleasure of the idyll and the "gentle" art. The great, popular, nineteenth-century literary genre of the *mystère*, the novel of the walk through the city, in France, primarily, opens into the walk as desolating and exposing, the mind loses rather than gains coherence and unity. It also, however, gains an exuberant sense of the infinite variety of human types and the unequal advantages bestowed upon them. Beginning, perhaps, with Restif de la Bretonne's *Les Nuits de Paris*, of the eighteenth century, this urban walking literature culminates in Baudelaire, Nerval, and surrealists like André Breton (*Nadja* and *L'amour fou*) and Louis Aragon (*Le Paysans de Paris*). Kafka's writing abounds in walking figures, and on numerous occasions in his letters he recounts his urban walks. The old central-European Jewish tale of *The Golem*, recently retold by Elie Wiesel (New York: Summit Books, 1983), is about a robotlike figure who with mystical physical strength looks to save the Jews from their ever-present Christian persecutors as he walks through the streets of Prague.

In English the gloom of the city walker appears in the early poetry of T. S. Eliot. New York City conforms more to the wistful imagination of Alfred Kazin in *A Walker in the City* (New York: Reynal & Hitchcock, 1948). No writer, however, walks through New York City glorying in the details of popular urban life and culture and full of desire more than the poet Frank O'Hara, unless it is the wonderful and often-neglected poet Charles Reznikoff. These writers bring an element of romance, of comfortable, lyric alienation, to the urban walk. Walter Benjamin, a superb walking essayist-as-sociologist-and-historian, presses for the dialectic between the Romantic, lyric imagination and sociological, politically motivated observation and critique. His walks through Berlin, Marseilles, Naples, and Moscow, and his historical reconstruction and critique of the Arcades of Paris in the nineteenth century for me fulfill the dialectic of walking—is simultaneous literary, visionary, psychological, and political tendencies. See *Reflections* and *Charles Baudelaire* (New York: Harcourt Brace Jovanovich, 1983). The walker Benjamin makes himself available to the city's assaults on the cultivated European imagination. Less elegant but as least as passionate is Ernesto Cardenal's long walking poem, "Trip to New York," in *Zero Hour* (New York: New Directions, 1980), a brilliant Whitmanesque poem of urban chaos and radical critique.

Walking fiction abounds. Aside from James Joyce's *Ulysses*, two of the most startling are Robert Walser's *The Walk*, in *The Walk and other stories*, trans. Christopher Middleton (London: John Calder, 1957) and Alex La Guma's *A Walk in the Night* (Evanston: Northwestern University Press, 1967). Walser, an older mid-European contemporary of Kafka, wrote a grimly comic meditation of a poor and alienated walker absorbed in friendly paranoid fantasies about the world through which he passes. La Guma's novella comes form the unrelenting world of South Africa's nonwhite urban oppressed whose only pitiful freedom and pleasure occur on the streets at night between their stops for cheap whiskey and the vicious cop's nightstick.

Both stories are to me masterpieces, a conviction—I'm sure—I hold because I discovered them unexpectedly in bookshops, with only my ever-attentive eye for walking literature directing me. In the extravagant poetic language of Breton, "A contact which wasn't even that for us, an involuntary contact with a single branch of the sensitive plant causes the meadow to shudder outside as inside us. We have nothing to do with it, or very little, and yet the whole expanse of grass bends down." *Mad Love*, trans. Mary Ann Caws (Lincoln: University of Nebraska Press, 1987), p. 84.

Just today I discovered Bruce Chatwin's latest book, *The Songlines* (New York: Viking, 1987), with the thesis that the wanderer is more comfortable with himself and his surroundings than is the sedentary person. Two quotations in this book caught my eye as I skimmed through it in the bookstore:

> Life is a bridge. Cross over it, but build no house on it.
>
> Indian Proverb

> You cannot travel on the path before you have become the path itself.
>
> Gautama Buddha